COMEDIENNES

D1403388

DISCARD

COMEDIENNES
Laugh be a Lady

DARRYL LITTLETON & TUEZDAE LITTLETON

Published in 2012 by Applause Theatre & Cinema Books
An Imprint of Hal Leonard Corporation
7777 West Bluemound Road
Milwaukee, WI 53213

Trade Book Division Editorial Offices
33 Plymouth St., Montclair, NJ 07042

Book design by Adam Fulrath

Printed in the United States of America

Library of Congress Cataloging-in-Publication Data

Littleton, Darryl.
 Comediennes : laugh be a lady / Darryl Littleton & Tuezdae Littleton.
    p. cm.
 Includes bibliographical references and index.
 ISBN 978-1-55783-842-1 (pbk.)
 1. Women comedians--United States--Biography. 2. Actresses--United States--Biography. I.
Littleton, Tuezdae. II. Title.
 PN2286.8.L58 2012
 792.702'8092--dc23
 [B]
                                    2012026875

www.applausebooks.com

Contents

Foreword

When asked to write this foreword, at first I was honored, then I panicked, and finally a peaceful resolve came over me. I know I was approached because I've been in the same trenches as the women in this book—I've mentored other comediennes and schooled countless audiences. I believe that all women are sisters, no matter what color, sexual preference, or religious affiliation. We are all sisters because we give birth to empires and nations.

Let me start by addressing the comediennes: although we fight the same war, our battles are somewhat different. Regardless, I say to you be your true selves. Tell your stories of love and woe. Some of you have had a lot of advantages— you came up in luxury and could've really afforded not to be comediennes. Others of you got into comedy as a way out of a lifestyle offering nothing more than a dead end. Either way, something inside all of us made us want to tell that truth. That's why I had to get this off my back. I had to tell that truth.

Stand-up has been one of the greatest gifts God ever gave to me outside of my children. It is my passion. It is my pain. It is my safe place against the world and my platform to tell my truth. The joy I feel in telling that truth is exhilaration. So I say this loud and proud to any comedienne reading: if you don't feel the same—get off my stage! A lot of women have fought to elevate us so you wouldn't have to get on your knees. A lot of comediennes have been belittled, many abused, so the art of female comedy could live on. Contemporary comediennes owe a huge debt to the women within these pages. Lord, the stories I could tell, but this book is a celebration.

So as a big sister in comedy I challenge all comediennes: perfect your art. Do it not only for yourselves, but for the reason we perform in the first place—for the audience.

Anybody reading this book will be able to see that the women from the past were consummate professionals. They paid their dues without complaint and paved the way for females to climb on stages, hit marks in films and television, and perform in all mediums available to women. The ability to make others laugh is a gift to be cherished. It shouldn't be played cheap or taken for granted. Comediennes have the power to change attitudes, alter perceptions, and even save lives. I love being a comedienne and can think of no higher calling. So to all comediennes and lovers of female comedy, God bless you all. Know that I love each and every one of you.

Thea Vidale

Thea Vidale is the first African American comedienne with a network show—Thea—named after her.

Preface

When I completed my first book, *Black Comedians on Black Comedy,* I felt I'd chronicled the most oppressed group in comedy. Then I met and married a comedienne and discovered just how many similarities blacks and females shared. When it comes to comedy, they had a staring contest on the bottom rung of the ladder.

However, it wasn't just comedy. Each group had to gain the vote through a constitutional amendment. Both women and blacks were portrayed by white men onstage until the authentic was requested and supplied. Both still find themselves filtered through a narrow funnel before a select few can claim success.

In each group, there are immovable shining examples and yardsticks that newcomers are measured by. Even the great Bernie Mac was told, "You ain't no Richard Pryor." Females have to live under the shadow of Lucille Ball. That last fact is quite disturbing when you take into account that Lucy was not technically a comedienne. She was an actress versed in a variety of genres. That she's best known for comedy is a tribute and testament to her and a detriment to the art of comedy.

The problem with females in comedy is they were even more oppressed than blacks. This became startling clear when I Googled the word "comedienne" and was directed to the more common term "comedian." Even in the cyber world the ladies were being dissed. The word I sought co·me·di·enne /[kuh-mee-dee-en], was French, a noun; defined as "a woman who is a comic entertainer or actress" and had its origin circa 1855.

Another difference between the two groups is that African American humorists can be traced with a line of succession. However, who are considered the female counterparts to Dick Gregory, Bill Cosby, Richard Pryor, Eddie Murphy, or Chris Rock? And has there ever been a female version of Lenny Bruce, Robert Klein, or George Carlin? So due to a dearth of major and influential stage comediennes, the definition has been expanded to include comedy actresses. There was no need to quibble—funny in any medium is funny.

Anyway, life is shorter the older you get and I just had my second daughter twenty years after my first. I realized I'm a girl producer and decided I wanted to produce something for the girls. So for the ladies in my life and around the world, I offer the tales of your yardsticks, women who gave their all to make us all better. I'm proud that my wife, Tuezdae, joined me in this journey and hope all who read our efforts view these ladies of laughter through renewed and appreciative eyes.

—Darryl Littleton

I've often wanted to change the bulb onstage just for women so that the spotlight was a little brighter. After all a lady deserves to shine.

Then I wondered if blinding people would be considered funny.

Few would get the humor, and the plague would continue to spread that women just aren't that funny.

Years ago when I was new to stand-up, I had no idea that I'd too often exposed my frustration with how women are treated, discounted, and disregarded in this male-dominated profession called comedy. Even the introduction is lousy: "Are you ready for a female?"; how about "Are you ready to keep the show going?" The audience will see the difference.

Many times women are just thrown into the mix as a breather in a tense room, just to lighten things up a bit; they're a means of intermission—use the restroom, get a drink, grab a smoke, or take that phone call outside.

In every way possible not to be taken seriously.

The hardest thing a woman has to do in comedy is be taken seriously.

So a big shout out to all the women of comedy who have performed on a stage, TV, radio, film, or in night clubs. You have enforced the truth that humor is a huge part of enjoying life and everyday relationships, so laugh with us because we are funny!

—Tuezdae Littleton

Acknowledgments

Thanks to All the Participating Talent

Adele Givens
Aida Rodriguez
Ajai Sanders
Alycia Cooper
Beth Payne
B-Phlat
Cocoa Brown
Di Stanky
Dominique
Edwonda White
Felicia Michaels
G-Mama Lee
Henrietta
Hope Flood
Iva La'Shawn
Jentle Phoenix
Jill Anenberg
Jus June Stubbs-Boykins
Kym Whitley
Laura Hayes
Loni Love
Luenell
Melanie Comarcho
Monique Marvez
Myra J
Nichelle Murdock
Nikki Carr
Nora Dunn
Olivia Arrington
Robin Montague
Rosie Tran
Sara Contreras
Shayla Rivera
Simply Marvelous
Sylvia Traymore Morrison
Thea Vidale
Vanessa Fraction
Vanessa Graddick

CHAPTER 1

Ladies-in-Waiting

"Being a funny person does an awful lot of things to you. You feel that you mustn't get serious with people. They don't expect it from you, and they don't want to see it. You're not entitled to be serious, you're a clown." —**Fanny Brice**

There was once a time men had to dress like women. They did it for no other reason than women were not allowed to do it themselves. On the theatrical stage, a female wasn't deemed competent enough to portray the depth and complexity of a woman. That was a job for a man, of course. Women belonged in the kitchens and bedrooms, not on stages for all to see. The only ladies out on the streets at night were ladies of the night, and the streets were their place of business. No respectable female would dwell in the wee hours for the entertainment of others.

Each culture broke this barrier at different times. Women did not appear on ancient stages. It wasn't until the advent of Christianity that a woman played a prominent role in comedy. In a tucked-away convent on the banks of the river Ganda in Germany lived a nun named Hrovithat (or Hrosvitha) (c. 935–973) or more commonly known as "The Nun of Gandersheim." She wrote a half dozen "comedies." They were tragic comedies, but this was as light as it was going to get in the politically divided, religiously upheaved tenth century. There's little known about her personal life, except that she died at the convent and ushered in the era (at the convent anyway) where women were allowed to perform her works (written in Latin) onstage. The nuns presented these comedies before the Bishop of Hildesheim and high officials of the empire. This practice of women performing in convents, though frowned upon by many bishops, was common up until the sixteenth century, most notably in Spain.

Non-nuns had to wait longer. It wasn't until the early sixteenth century that women were permitted on professional stages. This was in Spain, even though a special edict had been passed against it by Charles V. It didn't matter. Traveling troupes thumbed their noses to the quasi-law and women played women all around the countryside. In Cervantes's version of *Don Quixote,* the author's wife played the queen.

Circa 1586, Italian companies had women in their road performances. Marie Vernier was the first woman to grace a stage in France in 1548, after which regular theater with females took hold. In England, our British cousins could make fun of king and kingdom, but the queen in the play had a bulge until *Siege of Rhodes* introduced Mrs. Coleman to the Brits, whereas, S. Jordan, who'd written for the production of *Othello,* boldly stated that Mrs. Ann Marshall was the first. In Poland, a female first showed up at the beginning of the seventeenth century. The irony of Germany was that even though it was where Hrosvitha started it all, no lady performed there professionally until 1678. The origins of female stage infiltration from many other cultures remain ambiguous.

In America, comedy for women is different. The antics of humorists in the states is not what cracked them up in the courts of the kings or the tribal gatherings of the chiefs. By the time women were allowed to even plant their diminutive feet onstage, they were mainly deriving laughs from cute lyrics and broad, slap-sticky situations.

The minstrel era, originating circa 1830, was male dominated, and initially by white males in blackface. That is, until the Civil War broke out and many of those burnt cork appliers had to suit up for battle and leave the Negro stage shenanigans to actual Negroes. Even in this degrading age, women were not allowed to buffoon. The stereotype of the mammy was played by stout men, and the wench was portrayed by plump-shouldered young boys with small hands and feet. However, in 1870, impresario Michael B. Levitt founded Madame Rentz's Female Minstrels, an all-female troupe that performed in tights and skimpy outfits. They were very titillating for the day, to the point that in a San Francisco show minstrel named Mabel Shantley did a number where she raised her foot twelve inches and the audience went berserk. Before long, almost a dozen female minstrel troupes were touring, at least one having eliminated putting on blackface altogether. This trend gave way to the "girlie show," as they came to be known later.

However, it was the minstrel era that led to the first recognized comedienne, May Irwin, a product of the Rentz-Shantley Novelty and Burlesque Co.

May Irwin

Georgina May Campbell was born in 1862 in Ontario and started in show business with her sister, Flora, when they became fatherless and had to go to work. Billed as the Irwin Sisters, they lit up stages with their singing, dancing, and humorous patter. Debuting as an act in 1874, they were appearing at New York's Metropolitan Theater by 1877. The duo was a solid working team for the next six years, but in 1883, twenty-one-year-old May got antsy and decided to go solo. She joined Augustin Daly's stock company and for the next four years built a reputation for her improvisational abilities. May made her London debut in 1884, and by 1887, the more renowned Irwin moved on to work again with her sister, Flora, for the Rentz-Shantley Novelty and Burlesque Company.

The reunion of the Irwin Sisters was short-lived. Soon after Flora got mixed up in a murder scandal involving an amorous drifter, the ever-restless May went solo again and this time became a bona fide star on the vaudeville circuit, gaining notoriety for her "coon shouting," which was nothing more than doing African American–based songs. In 1895, she got the attention of Thomas Edison when she and co-star John C. Rice engaged in a long, lingering kiss during a number in the production of *The Widow Jones.* Edison had them repeat it for his 1896 film *The Kiss,* making it the first ever screen lip lock.

May got married in 1907 to her manager. The same year she started recording for Berliner / Victor. Her combination of buxom figure and charming personality kept Irwin a top star for over thirty years. So popular was May that during World War I, President Woodrow Wilson got a solo command performance so he could relieve the tension of the war with a few chuckles. He dubbed her "Secretary of Laughter." After that the door was not flung wide open for comediennes, but at least it was cracked.

Sophie Tucker

Sophie Tucker was also a "coon shouter." "The Last of the Red Hot Mamas" hired black singers (Ethel Waters was one) to teach her the proper way to deliver the material. She even employed an African American composer to write her songs. In 1909, the bawdy burlesque singer/comedienne played the Ziegfeld Follies, until the other female acts refused to work with her and she was let go. The lull didn't last long as the founder of the William Morris Agency, William Morris himself, booked Sophie into his American Music Hall. Due to theater owner pressure for her to look a certain way, Sophie wore blackface. One night she couldn't find her makeup and went onstage without it and was more of a smash than with it.

She never wore blackface again, but did keep black-influenced material as part of her act.

The Russian-Jewish Tucker was born on January 13, 1886, in Tulchyn, Ukraine. Her parents immigrated to Hartford, Connecticut, in the United States when she was too young to remember it, changed their names, and opened a restaurant. It was in the family business that Sophie began her singing career. She warbled for tips. In her seventeenth year, she married the first of her three husbands. None of those marriages lasted more than five years, including the one to Louis Tuck, but she did like the name and changed hers from Abuza (the name her parents chose to sound more American) to Tucker.

Unlike most female entertainers of the era, the risqué songs of Sophie Tucker played up her sexual desires—"Nobody Loves a Fat Girl but Oh How a Fat Girl Can Love." She recorded popular songs on Edison Records and performed to sold-out crowds for her personal appearances, where she and her accompanist, Ted Shapiro, engaged in naughty banter. Sophie played Judy Garland's mother in the film *Broadway Melody of 1938* and had her own self-titled radio show that same year. She was elected president of the American Federation of Actors after helping unionizing its membership, appeared on *The Ed Sullivan Show* and *The Tonight Show* in the '50s and '60s, and did shows until her death from lung cancer in 1966.

Fanny Brice

Fania Borach came from a well-off family, so she didn't need to get on stages and coax laughs from patrons as Fanny Brice. There were servants and trips overseas to visit relatives for the young girl, with funds derived from her family's string of profitable saloons in Newark, New Jersey. Even when her father slid into nonproductive alcoholism, a substantial income continued to flow in. Regardless, her mother left him, moved the children to Brooklyn, and became a successful real-estate agent. Poverty was a word to Fanny, scarcely a reality. Nothing in her background dictated a life in the spotlight. She had absolutely no reason to go into comedy, except that comedy chooses you, not the other way around.

Fanny answered the call. After dropping out of school to perform in burlesque shows, where she took on the name Brice, she eventually formed a relationship with Florenz Ziegfeld and was soon headlining the prestigious Ziegfeld Follies. However, prior to her lofty ascension she'd debuted on *Frank Kenney's Amateur Vaudeville* as a singer, been fired from a chorus by George M. Cohan for not being able to dance, and had broken into the professional ranks touring in a Shubert brothers production. Fanny appeared in the Follies from 1910 to 1911, then returned in 1921. During her career, she recorded hit songs, made movies, and created her claim to fame—*The Baby Snooks Show,* which made its debut in the Follies in 1933, two years after the death of Flo Ziegfeld. The character of a devilish yet basically good little girl was so popular, it was adapted for radio that same year and ran until her death in 1951.

Brice was forty-five years old when the Snooks era began, but she was compulsively devoted to her alter ego. She wore little girl attire whenever she recorded Snooks, even though the only people seeing this early form of method acting was a radio studio audience. So immersed in her work was Fanny that she remained in the Snooks mindset, minus the voice, for at least an hour after each performance. In an interview, Brice revealed that during the time she was Snooks, Fanny Brice ceased to exist. She loved her creation and justifiably thought everyone else felt the same. An ill-conceived attempt to bring the character to television quickly bombed, as a woman who'd been one for some time dressed as a little girl seemed odd and creepy, so back to radio Snooks went.

Brice was married three times: first to a barber named Frank White. That lasted a whopping three days, after it was discovered the trimmer had an appetite for the trim of young starlets. Her next husband was professional gambler Nick Arnstein, who she visited in Sing Sing every week for fourteen months. When he was released, they lived together for six months, got married, and he soon disappeared, so she divorced him. The last winner was songwriter Billy Rose. That union also failed. So she left no husband to mourn for her when she passed of a cerebral hemorrhage, but she did leave several portrayals of herself in film, the most notable being Barbra Streisand's Oscar-winning turn in *Funny Girl.*

JOSEPHINE BAKER

Fanny Brice might've wowed them at the Ziegfeld Follies, but that show obviously wasn't for everybody. Josephine Baker received poor reviews and was replaced by Gypsy Rose Lee. The Follies held a minority opinion for the dancer/ singer/comedienne. The rest of society loved Josephine Baker, especially her adopted homeland France. She became the first African American woman to integrate concert halls and star in a motion picture. She also held the distinction of being the highest paid chorus girl in vaudeville. Her routine included acting like she forgot the dance number and engaging in comedic banter for a while, trying to figure it out, and then performing the number flawlessly and with precision-perfect embellishments. Josephine first displayed her remarkable abilities during the Harlem Renaissance in shows such as 1921's *Shuffle Along* and *The Chocolate Dandies* in 1924.

Born in St. Louis in 1906, Josephine went to work at age eight. Unfortunately it was for a woman who abused her. At age twelve, she left school and lived on the streets, digging through garbage cans for food and sleeping in cardboard shelters. Her street dancing got her on vaudeville when she was fifteen and in the Folies Bergere in France before she was twenty. She wore a banana skirt, starred in successful French films, wrote hit songs, became a muse to the likes of Ernest Hemingway, Langston Hughes, and Christian Dior, spied for France during WWII with information gathered written in invisible ink on her sheet music, adopted twelve children of different nationalities, refused to perform for segregated audiences in the US, spoke at the 1963 March on Washington with Martin Luther King Jr. (the only woman to speak at the historic event), and was the first American woman to receive full French military honors at her funeral.

Josephine Baker died on April 12, 1975, at the age of sixty-eight after suffering a cerebral hemorrhage in her bedroom in Paris. Her remarkable career spanned fifty years and she made the most of every day. The one-time street urchin kicked open doors for women in performing onstage and removed barriers for women of color. She wasn't just a national treasure, but a gem of the world.

CHAPTER 2

The Better Halves

"When I was born I was so surprised I didn't talk for a year and a half." —**Gracie Allen**

The Ziegfeld Follies had Fanny Brice and Sophie Tucker (who until 1909 appeared onstage in blackface when she performed because theater owners told her she was too fat and ugly to show up any other way) for comic relief. Minstrel shows were still touring the countryside, and vaudeville was struggling but still alive in the '20s. The era known as the Roaring Twenties hadn't advanced feminine comedy much, but the prospects for women advanced by leaps and bonds. The country was obsessed with success, and optimism was bubbling over in every corner of society.

World War I (aka the Great War) had Americans pushing their chests out. With the help of our allies, we'd defeated the original Evil Empire and now it was time to celebrate. The country sang songs, drank heavily, and made love quietly and discreetly. The League of Nations, though a noble idea, was a dismal failure, and Woodrow Wilson's legacy lay more in the winning of a war so huge the word "World" had to be attached. Entertainment provided a variety of distractions. There was the magic and escape escapades of Harry Houdini, and the operatic vocal artistry of Enrico Caruso; athletes the likes of Babe Ruth and Jack Dempsey graced the national headlines; and the movie houses were packed whenever Tom Mix, Fatty Arbuckle, Charlie Chaplin, Harold Lloyd, Douglas Fairbanks, or the genteel Mary Pickford appeared onscreen.

In the early 1920s, husband-and-wife comedy teams provided several comediennes with the opportunity to work regularly. The duo of Stringbean and Sweetie Pie were a smash hit on the TOBA (Theater Owners Bookers Association) chitlin circuit tours. Their act was heavy on the song and dance and light on the comedy. Then tragedy struck and Stringbean (Budd LeMay) died. The promoter wasted no time in replacing the crowd favorites. Jodie and Susie Edwards got the gig.

The Edwards were in the right place at the right time. Jodie, born in 1895, had started out as a dancer. Susie Hawthorne, born in 1896, worked her craft in black theater. They met in 1916, and like true performers got married onstage. It wasn't until 1920 that they performed as a duo, thanks to the passing of Stringbean. They had been opening shows for the team doing their respective acts when the promoter came to Jodie and asked him to change his name to "Butterbeans" and put together a husband-and-wife act with Susie (who was able to keep her real name).

BUTTERBEANS and SUSIE

B utterbeans and Susie were more about comedy than singing and dancing. Susie dressed in refined attire and Butterbeans played the fool. So they used the dichotomy to amp up the comedy. They quarreled like a couple, talked risqué like a couple, and ribbed each other like a couple. Butterbeans would even threaten to whoop Susie's ass, but he was such a ridiculous sight (too-small pants, bow tie, bowler hat, floppy shoes) that such effronteries were played strictly for laughs. Translation—they were a smash hit (with everybody except the old-fashioned crowd). It wasn't long before they moved on to vaudeville and toured with a blackface minstrel troupe, the Rabbit's Foot Company. They recorded blues songs and starred in an early black movie.

Butterbeans and Susie destroyed stages across the country. They had signature songs like "A Married Man's a Fool If He Thinks His Wife Don't Love Nobody but Him" and the even more suggestive "I Want a Hot Dog for My Roll." That one was so dirty even their record label, Okeh, wouldn't release it.

Wonder why. The lyrics seemed harmless enough:

I want a hot dog for my bread you see
'Cause I carry my bread with me.
I want it hot, I don't want it cold
I want it so it fit my roll"

While Susie danced salaciously to the tune, Butterbeans would interject lines such as "My dog's never cold" and "Here's a dog that's long and lean." What's the problem?

The act would climax with a song showing that the couple really loved each other, and then Butterbeans would perform "The Itch," where he'd shove his hands into his pockets and start scratching feverishly until he'd pull them out of his pockets and scratch his whole body. The audiences went nuts for this bit.

They were crowd-pleasers as well as patrons of their art and helped many other acts of the era. It was Butterbeans and Susie that introduced Moms Mabley to a broader audience.

GRACIE ALLEN

It's common knowledge that most women don't like to discuss their age, but nobody knows when Gracie Allen was born. Not even her husband, George Burns, knew. That's because Gracie was born in San Francisco. That city's famous 1906 earthquake and subsequent fire destroyed most of its records, including births. Thus few inhabitants from that time period have an accurate accounting of their origins. Grace

Ethel Cecile Rosalie Allen is one of them. Some accounts have her birth year as early as 1895, others as late as 1906. All we know for sure is that she was three when she first hit the stage, got a break from Eddie Cantor on his broadcast *On Air*, performed Irish folk dances with the Four Colleens, which consisted of her and her three sisters. She then became a vaudeville entertainer in 1909 with her sister Bessie, met George Burns in 1922, and soon after they formed a comedy duo and after a lengthy courtship got married in 1927.

The comedy pairing of Burns and Allen was classic straight man/funny man, except Gracie was the straight man. The original act had Burns hitting the punch lines, but Allen's setups were getting more laughs than the jokes. So Burns wisely changed the act around, and with Gracie saying all the funny lines, they became vaudeville headliners. All Burns had to do was ask her a question and let her combination of innocence, zaniness, and stupidity rattle on to waves of laughter. The real Gracie was a very intelligent person, but aren't most entertainers who play dumb?

By the early '30s they'd moved into radio. The problem was the youthful flirting of their vaudeville shows didn't mesh with their advancing ages, so Burns adjusted the act again to be more married-couple oriented, albeit a show biz married couple. Now it was about Gracie doing dumb things and her hapless husband trying to work around them.

They did movies—two films with W. C. Fields (1933's *International House* and 1934's *Six of a Kind*) and *A Damsel in Distress* with Fred Astaire. The latter deserves mentioning because it was the first movie Astaire did without dance partner Ginger Rogers. However, Burns and Allen were experienced dancers from vaudeville and astounded film goers when they kept up with the greatest movie dancer step for step.

Burns and Allen also became known for their inventive publicity stunts. In 1932, the gag was Gracie was looking for her brother. They popped up on shows of other performers, asking, "Has anybody seen Gracie's brother?" Her real-life brother, in the meanwhile, found that the running joke had gotten so widespread that he had to go into hiding for several weeks until it blew over. Another stunt had Gracie running for president. She represented the Surprise Party, gave speeches, and in the 1940 general election got 42,000 votes. They also ribbed the upper-crust set when Gracie performed a piano concerto at Carnegie Hall. The bit was having the orchestra play, then pause so Gracie could hit a single note for her solo section. The note was always a wrong note, until her final solo where the correct note was played to the thunderous applause of the orchestra and the conductor.

Their move to television came in 1948, at the prompting of colleague and friend Jack Benny. He'd moved his radio show from NBC to CBS because the latter network was more talent friendly. So now the formula Burns and Allen used for radio was adapted to TV, with the same successful results. In 1958, Gracie retired due to health reasons after their eighth season. George Burns tried to keep the show going, and it was renamed *The George Burns Show,* but the viewing audience made it clear that it was the "without Gracie we're not watching show." It came to an end after one low-rated season.

Burns and Allen came to represent the ideal couple— publicly. Privately Gracie had issues with her appearance. She'd been scarred severely as a child after being accidentally scalded and wore long sleeves to hide the marks on her arm. It became known as the Gracie Allen style. She had to swim in the family's swimming pool to prove to their adopted two children that she could actually swim. Gracie was also sensitive because they couldn't conceive children together and was also annoyed because she had one green eye and one blue eye. She feared being exposed if the show ever went to color. The one thing that didn't seem to bother Gracie is when Burns cheated on her after they argued about the cost of a coffee table. George Burns told Jack Benny about his Vegas showgirl indiscretion, not knowing Gracie overheard him. Out of guilt, he bought her the expensive coffee table she desired. However, instead of reprimanding him for stepping out of the marriage, she told a friend that she wished he'd cheat more often. She could use the furniture.

Following her retirement, Gracie Allen stayed out of the public eye as she battled heart disease. She finally succumbed in 1964 and passed from heart failure. George Burns was laid by her side when he died thirty-two years later. Their marker reads, "Gracie Allen and George Burns—Together Again."

CHAPTER 3

Never Give a Sucker Anything

"I generally avoid temptation unless I can't resist it." —**Mae West**

Everybody was making money. Everybody was spending money. Nobody could be told it would end. Yet it did. Like all good things, the good times came to a screeching halt. For almost a decade prosperity had ruled the countryside. Hunger? Isn't that something they have in foreign countries? Here in the land of milk and honey, we have a surplus of both. The only thing to worry about is if that bastard Hoover will ever stop treating folks like children and relax.

Republican Herbert Hoover had won a landslide victory over Democratic presidential rival Al E. Smith, who was against the Volstead Act. That's how they got him. That and the fact that he was Catholic. In 1928, attacking Smith for the last fact was considered in poor political taste, but calling him a drunken anti-Prohibitionist was just fine, and that's what the Hoover camp along with the Women's Christian Temperance Union did to poor Al Smith. The result—the secret drinker and hypocrite (he'd go to the Belgium Embassy—considered foreign soil and not affected by US law—after work to chug a few down), Herbert Clark Hoover took over the US and its future.

Some future. Prior to Hoover, the former commerce secretary with no elected office experience, taking over, it was one big decade-long party. All Prohibition had done was to make drinking sexier and gangsters richer. It was after World War I and the nation was giddy. We'd won and now it was time to celebrate. Consumers consumed and it was a period of tremendous economic growth. Radios were the hottest things out and urbanization reached its peak. It was the time of the Jazz Age, the Harlem Renaissance, Mickey Mouse and Felix the Cat cartoons, speakeasies and underworld figures named Al and Bugsy, Art Deco design, "flappers," drunken sex orgies, the Lindy Hop, Valentino, Clara Bow, and Al Jolson. It was the time of the nation's life.

It was a time of women's suffrage. On August 18, 1920, Tennessee became the last of thirty-six states needed to ratify the Nineteenth Amendment, granting women the right to vote. Equality at the polls marked a pivotal moment in the women's rights movement. It meant a reassessment of the role of women in modern society. They could have a career and a family. They could make more money. They could freely admit they had sexual urges just like men, and like men, it was destructive to suppress them. They could proclaim themselves sexual beings.

Then came October 24, 1929—"Black Thursday." There had been warnings from noted economists, unheeded by the new president, who felt everything was fine. The country was in a bull market. Well, the optimism of that bull market shattered, share prices on the NYSE collapsed, and stock prices plummeted. Enter the Great Depression. Bread lines. Soup kitchens. Families being evicted and put out on the streets.

Most would've felt that following the stock market crash of '29, making sexy funny would've been no small task, but then again Mae West was no small woman. Like the era, Mary Jane West also felt like it was too soon for the party to be over. Her father had been a prizefighter who became a private detective. Her mother was a corset model who claimed to be Protestant, but was really Jewish; whereas her paternal grandfather was an African American passing for white. Whatever the case—Mary just wanted to have fun.

MAE WEST

Mae West was like all good things we desire: started early and ended late. Her first performance was at a church social of all places. She was five years old. After paying her dues doing amateur contests and winning talent shows, Mary Jane began her professional career at the ripe old age of fourteen, performing under the stage name Baby Mae. She tried a lot of different incarnations—blackface coon shouter and even a female impersonator. It was said that her signature walk was inspired by a couple of drag queens.

The year 1911 was big for West. She married fellow vaudevillian Frank Wallace (four years her senior) and did her first play on Broadway. The show folded after eight performances and the marriage was kept a secret. Mae was trying to get a name as a sex symbol and being known as a married lady would only cramp her style. This would've been fine except for Guido Deiro, another vaudevillian West met and allegedly married around 1914, while still also secretly married to Wallace. Bigamy, schmigamy—let the courts catch her and figure all that out. She had a career to cultivate. On her next project, she worked with Al Jolson (whom she did not marry) in *Vera Violetta*.

Mae's mother loved her rise in show business, but other members of the West clan weren't as enthusiastic over Mae's chosen career and high-kicking lifestyle. The aunt who delivered her into the world and various other women in the family flat out resented it. What she was doing on those stages, in front of all those people, well, decent women just didn't do those types of things. She was a model on the sheet music for the suggestive dance "The Shimmie," for heaven's sake.

By 1916, West made a major change in her life. Mae had gotten pregnant by Guido Deiro and aborted the child without telling him, suffering complications that put her down for a year. She and Guido split around that same time (officially filing for divorce in 1920 for adultery). Then, in 1918, Mae got her big break, co-starring with Ed Wynn in the Shubert brothers revue *Sometime*. That success encouraged West to write her own risqué plays under the pen name Jane Mast. The result was *Sex*. She not only wrote it, but produced, directed, and starred. She also got arrested for it. Seems the local city officials didn't care for that type of production in their jurisdiction, and Mae West was sentenced to ten days in jail for "corrupting the morals of youth." She served eight days with two days off for good behavior. Good is right. She dined with the Warden and his wife while incarcerated and wore silk underwear (not necessarily standard-issue attire).

Having survived her harrowing experience behind bars, Mae West was the talk of the town. The media could hardly wait for her next outing, and they didn't have to wait long. It was a play she penned entitled *Drag,* which dealt with homosexuality. Mae herself was a vocal advocate of gay rights, but the subject matter of the production was just a tad bit too rough for the Society for the Prevention of Vice. Their threat to ban it if she attempted a Broadway run left *Drag* out in the cold.

West wrote other controversial plays (*The Wicked Age, Pleasure Man, The Constant Sinner*) that all ensured media coverage and packed houses of curious audiences. However, it was her 1928 production, *Diamond Lil,* that forced her out of Broadway. In the play, she had the persona that would define her: the hot-to-trot wise-cracking she-devil. The play was a smash hit and allowed West the leverage she desired. It was so popular that she could revive it anytime she wanted to and get the same awesome results.

Thanks to the overwhelming success of *Diamond Lil,* Mae West was off to Hollywood in 1932. Paramount Studios made her an offer and she gladly accepted. She was thirty-eight years old (which she kept quiet), but that didn't matter. Mae was determined to cement her buxom man-eater persona into the culture. The way she saw it, Tinsel Town would be just another nut to crack, another frontier to conquer—and it was. Not only did she steal scenes from more established stars like George Raft in her debut film, *Night After Night,* West also crafted her own dialogue. Raft later said, "She stole everything but the cameras."

Mae was ambitious and trying to make up for lost time. She moved into screenwriting. She also dabbled a bit in casting when she spotted a relatively unknown Cary Grant and selected him for her film *She Done Him Wrong,* a big career boost for Grant and a savior for Paramount Studios, which was on the brink of bankruptcy. This movie was not only a box office hit, it received an Academy Award nomination for Best Picture. Her 1933 movie, *I'm No Angel* (co-starring Cary Grant again), was yet another blockbuster. Mae was now a major player. She was so popular that her many suggestive quotes became part of the lexicon:

"It's not the men in your life that count, it's the life in your men."

"Marriage is a great institution, but I'm not ready for an institution."

"When I'm good, I'm very good, but when I'm bad, I'm better."

"Is that a gun in your pocket, or are you just glad to see me?"

By 1935, this icon-in-the-making was earning more than any other person in the country, with the exception of newspaper mogul William Randolph Hearst.

Then tragedy: on July 1, 1934, censorship threatened to

lay siege to the Mae West empire. The Production Code was finally being taken seriously and her screenplays came under intense scrutiny. Editing was the task of the day. Her 1934 film, *Belle of the Nineties,* was originally titled *It Ain't No Sin.* Audiences thought it was because they weren't too crazy about it. *Goin' to Town,* in 1935, got mixed reviews from critics. Several more films followed, but with heavy censorship and a lackluster box office, Paramount cut West loose in 1937.

What does a fallen movie star do to pay the bills? Radio. West appeared on ventriloquist Edgar Bergen's program and flirted with his dummy, Charlie McCarthy. She said things like how he was all wood and a yard long. This was racy in the day and the complaints from Catholic groups, who already had it in for her, came pouring into the station. Another sketch on that same show had her playing Eve to Don Ameche's Adam, and it was deemed so suggestive that it was one of the first times the FCC got involved. Mae West wasn't allowed on radio again until 1950.

It was back to the silver screen: 1940's *My Little Chickadee,* co-starring comedian W. C. Fields. It was a Universal Studios picture and it was fraught with problems from the outset. One was the fact that they couldn't stand each other. Another was battles over the screenplay. The end result, though, was a box-office smash. Unfortunately Mae wasn't so lucky in love or business. In 1942, she gained a legal divorce from her secret husband, Frank Wallace, and in 1943 *The Heat's On* for Columbia Pictures was released. Something told her not to touch this turkey, but producer/director Greg Ratoff begged her and lied about going under if she didn't. In other words, she was his only hope. So like the trooper she was, Mae made the sniveling man's movie and faced the wrath of everybody when it turned out to be a box-office disaster. She didn't make another film for thirty-seven years.

Before the stench of *The Heat's On* dissipated, West was back on Broadway in *Catherine Was Great,* a spoof produced by Mike Todd. It ran for almost two hundred performances, demonstrating that Mae West wasn't passé.

She just had to be uncensored. Besides Broadway, Las Vegas offered similar freedom, so Mae mounted her own stage play surrounded by big, hulking hunks and kept the sex goddess image alive. Accordingly she had a new man in her life, former Mr. California Chester Rybonski. They lived together until her death. It was also around this time that she was approached about another movie, Billy Wilder's *Sunset Boulevard,* but she said no. In an interview, Wilder said it was for the best. West was too much like the character Norma Desmond. She actually thought she was still as hot and sexy as ever at age fifty-seven.

By the '60s, the one-time sex symbol was popping up on television. West made appearances on *The Red Skelton Show* and *Mr. Ed* spoofing herself. Then in a feeble attempt to stay relevant with the younger audience, she recorded a rock-and-roll album, covering songs by the Doors and others. In 1970, she co-starred with reigning sex queen Raquel Welch in the bomb *Myra Breckenridge* and later worked on *Sextette.* This last film found her disoriented and required director Ken Hughes to shoot her from the waist up so audiences wouldn't see the assistant leading her around to her marks during filming.

In 1980, Mae West was hospitalized after falling out of bed. She'd suffered a stroke, then another one that paralyzed her right side. After it was determined there was nothing further medical science could do, West was sent home, where she passed away at age eighty-seven on November 22, 1980.

Mae West had been a powerful cultural force in the 1930s. She was the reigning queen of sex and innuendo in stage, screen, and broadcasting, a toxic blend of public curiosity and repulsion. Those elements were her triumphs and her defeats. Predicting what a mass audience will accept and appreciate has always been a crap shoot at best, so Mae never even tried. Like most true entertainers, she gave them what she liked and waited to see who followed. She had enough traipsing behind her to fill her sizable coffers.

CAROLE LOMBARD

O n the flip side, beautiful and spirited Carole Lombard was also pulling down some big bucks during the Great Depression. She was the queen of screwball comedies in the '30s and early '40s. The nation was reeling from record unemployment and anxiety over the future. The new president, Franklin Delano Roosevelt, had defeated outgoing Leader of the Free World Herbert Hoover on promises of a better direction for America and an administration that would pull the country out of its financial nosedive. Part of that new attitude had to start with each and every American pulling themselves out of the doldrums and keeping their heads held high. Easy to say when you're eating, also when you're laughing. And when times are hard, comedy is the best distraction to keep an angry mob from storming the walls and lynching their leaders. So in the ensuing years there was no shortage of merry makers.

Born in 1908, Lombard (born Jane Alice Peters) spent the early part of her life growing up in Fort Wayne, Indiana. Life was idyllic for the tomboy in the two-story family home. It was until her father was injured at work, leaving him with headaches so severe he'd burst into fits of anger without warning. This was more than Carole's mother could bear, and she packed up her little girl and her two older brothers, Fred and Stuart, and moved to Los Angeles in 1914. There Carole attended Virgil Junior High and Fairfax High, where she dropped out after being elected May Queen and pursued acting, getting her GED years later.

Lombard was a product of silent films, making her debut at age twelve and billed as Jane Peters. Following several small parts in even smaller pictures, her friendship with noted director Raoul Walsh's wife, Miriam Cooper, gave her career a much needed boost. She changed her name to Lombard and got signed as a contract player with Fox Film Corporation. After working with comedy impresario Mack Sennett, Lombard gained the reputation of being a funny presence on-screen, and when "talkies" took over was signed to a contract by Paramount Pictures. Her rapid-fire delivery was made to order.

For some time Lombard was little more than a typical, pretty B-movie actress. However, she found a way to pass the time until her big break came along by getting married to reserved, urbane actor William Powell. Friends thought them an odd pair. Besides, the sixteen-year age difference, which Lombard stated repeatedly, did not matter; It was their differences in personality. She was loud, rambunctious, and outgoing, and he was not. Ah, friends. Lombard's turned out to be right. The Powell–Lombard marriage last a whopping two years, after which Lombard moved into a bachelorette pad and became known as the hostess with the mostest, throwing wild parties and dating actors Gary Cooper and George Raft. She was having a grand old time, but her career was going nowhere. Unlike the versatile Mae West, Lombard was strictly a film comedienne; no stage experience, no writing ambitions, no radio. So it was stand in front of a camera or party.

An encounter at a party changed all that when she met Howard Hawks, who liked her personality and cast her opposite theater legend/voluminous drinker John Barrymore in the classic *Twentieth Century.* Things were looking up. Several films later, she received the starring role in 1936's *My Man Godfrey,* co-starring former husband William Powell as a bum turned butler (every ex-wife's dream). Lombard was nominated for a Best Actress Oscar. This led to *Nothing Sacred* in 1937, a box-office winner that put her in the rarefied air of top-paid stars in Hollywood—hilarity to the tune of a half-million dollars average in the late '30s (more than the US president).

All the accolades and money made Carole Lombard a serious actress. Too bad she took the serious part to heart. Her next several films were dramas that few Lombard fans embraced. Audiences quickly reminded her that she was strictly there for laughs. Part of her need for pathos might have been her personal life. She'd fallen in love with screen titan Clark Gable, who was unhappily married at the time to an oil heiress. Gable was big at the box office, but not personally at the bank. He needed money to settle his divorce, and crafty MGM head, Louis B. Mayer, provided it. Since Gable had been reluctant to play Rhett Butler in Mayer's proposed epic *Gone with the Wind,* Louis made sure he'd have enough dough to get out of his marriage and live his life. During the filming of *Gone with the Wind,* the two lovebirds drove to Arizona and were wed.

Life was good for the Gables. They had pet names for each other ("Ma" and "Pa") and bought a ranch in Encino, where they raised horses and chickens. Unfortunately no children, but not that they didn't try. The two made each other extremely happy. So much so that Lombard triumphantly returned to her comedy roots with Alfred Hitchcock's *Mr. and Mrs. Smith* and *To Be or Not to Be* with Jack Benny.

While the latter picture was still in post-production, America entered World War II following the bombing of Pearl Harbor. Lombard might have been a foul-mouth party hostess and screwball comedy starlet, but she was also a patriot. Doing her part, she went to her home state of Indiana on a successful war-bond rally. After raising over $2 million, she boarded a plane bound for California and her loving man back home. The flight never made it. After refueling in Las Vegas, the plane slammed into the side of a mountain and all twenty-two passengers were killed instantly, including Gable's press agent and Lombard's mother, Bess Peters. Gable was inconsolable and joined the US Air Force, flying five missions himself. His beautiful bride was dead at age thirty-three.

The tragic death of Carole Lombard rocked Hollywood and the nation. The premature demise of a career filled with such promise was disturbing, to say the least. In contrast, African Americans in the United States were used to living with disturbances. Jim Crow laws in the South prevented many from living out their basic promise and an overall climate of bigotry hampered most. For black females in show business in the '30s, the road was rougher than their white counterparts, and the line of reality and fantasy remained blurred.

HATTIE McDANIEL

Hattie McDaniel was a songwriter, singer, and actress, as well as a comedienne (and carries the distinction of being the very first African American female to perform on radio). The future Oscar winner had a highly successful radio show where she played Hi-Hat Hattie, the maid who often forgot her place, but in the real world she was making a wage so low that she had to work as a real maid when not recording the show.

She was born in Wichita, Kansas, in 1895, the child of former slaves. The family moved to Colorado, and Hattie's brother, Sam, jumped into the entertainment world as a minstrel. Hattie soon followed and honed her songwriting skills working on his show. She expanded her career by singing on a local radio station in Denver and recording several records for Okeh Records and Paramount Records in Chicago. Then the stock market crash of '29 hit and all that came to a screeching halt. McDaniel was forced to work as a bathroom attendant and waitress at Club Madrid in Milwaukee, where she was eventually allowed to take the stage and perform.

In 1931, McDaniel joined Sam in Los Angeles. There she found radio work and appeared in a number of uncredited film parts, including a small role in the Mae West film *I'm No Angel*. She played a plump maid. In 1934, she joined the Screen Actors Guild and got other parts as maids when she wasn't working as a real one to make ends meet. In 1937, she was employed on Carole Lombard's film *Nothing Sacred,* and while working on MGM's *China Seas* she met Clark Gable, who would become a friend and ally.

During this period, the black community lashed out at McDaniel for taking maid roles. No matter how sassy the maids she played were, blacks didn't like it. Oddly enough, it was also around this time that casting began for the much

publicized *Gone with the Wind.* The movie was to be adapted
from Margaret Mitchell's bestselling book and Mammy was
a coveted role. It was so in demand that President Roosevelt's
wife, Eleanor, asked the studio to let her personal maid play it.
Clark Gable insisted on McDaniel. Leaving nothing to chance,
she went to the audition dressed in a traditional maid's
uniform and got the part.

Getting the role was one thing, being able to watch her
work at the premiere was another. Gone *with the Wind* made
its debut in Atlanta, Georgia. None of the black actors from
the film were invited to attend. As a matter of fact, they were
expressly told not to attend. Clark Gable heatedly refused to
go under those circumstances. That is until McDaniel pulled
him to the side, thanked him for his friendship and loyalty,
but informed him that she wasn't surprised and he needed to
go to promote the film. She'd make the Hollywood premiere.
Reluctantly Gable relented and made the journey to Georgia.

For her troubles, Hattie McDaniel was the first African
American to be nominated for an Academy Award and the
first to win (for Best Supporting Actress). In her speech, she
graciously thanked the Academy for the honor, and sporting
pulled back hair laced in gardenias, expressed her gratitude
and thanked God. Many in attendance were moved to tears.
Her friendship with Gable extended beyond the movie set.
When McDaniel protested redlining practices in the West
Adams Heights district of Los Angeles and won, making the
area available for qualified blacks to occupy, it was the king of
Hollywood who consistently attended her house parties.

Following *Gone with the Wind,* McDaniel played other
maid parts in films starring Bette Davis and Humphrey
Bogart, and worked under the direction of John Huston. She
always turned in fine performances and received glowing
reviews. However, by the late 1940s, the place for domestics
on-screen was becoming passé. Regardless, McDaniel stayed
busy on radio and later in television, starring in *Beulah* (both
mediums), where she earned $2,000 per week. She'd taken over
from Ethel Waters after the first season of the show, but after

discovering she had breast cancer, McDaniel had to bow out
and was herself replaced by Louise Beavers.

Hattie McDaniel died in 1952 from breast cancer at the age
of fifty-seven. Her wish was to be buried in the Hollywood
Cemetery, but that wish was denied by the owner, Jules Roth,
because black people were not allowed there. So she found a
final resting home at Rosedale Cemetery. She left no spouse,
even though she'd been married four times. The first marriage
ended when her husband died. The second lasted less than
a year. The third dissolved after a false pregnancy threw
her into a depression and her husband grew jealous of her
career and threatened to kill her. The fourth was destroyed by
arguing and fighting and lasted about a year. Then in 1999,
the Hollywood Cemetery, under new owner Tyler Cassity,
reversed its decision, but it was too late. The family refused to
have her remains moved, so to make amends Cassity built a
memorial at the Hollywood Cemetery in McDaniel's honor.

DARLA HOOD

Another female member of a minority being held back in
this period was Darla Hood, of *Our Gang* fame. Born
Darla Jean Hood on November 4, 1931, this coquettish child
was overshadowed in the '30s by the much more famous and
accomplished Shirley Temple, who could sing, dance, and
tell a boatload of jokes with charisma exploding from her
dimples. Hood could do all of that minus the dimples. At the
age of three her mother took her from Oklahoma to New York
City, where she was seen by a Hal Roach Studios casting
director and whisked off to California to play in the *Our Gang*
comedies.

She began her *Our Gang* stint in 1935, playing the
"girlfriend" of head-over-heels Alfalfa and the well-to-do
Waldo. In these lighthearted shorts, she'd get the opportunity
to show where her parent's money went for singing and
dancing lessons. In "The Pinch Singer," Hood got to croon
"I'm in the Mood for Love." Her tenure with the gang ended

in 1941, but that didn't put a stop to her career. Hood had an impressive film and recording output, headlining her own show at the Coconut Grove, Copacabana, and the Sahara Hotel in Las Vegas, as well as appearing regularly on Edgar Bergen's radio program. She also did voice-overs and sang on commercials for Chicken of the Sea and Campbell Soup, among others.

The tragedy of Darla Hood is how she died. While organizing the Little Rascals [the later name of *Our Gang*] reunion in 1980, she went to the hospital for what should have been a minor procedure. Instead she contracted acute hepatitis and died unexpectedly of heart failure at the age of forty-seven on June 13, 1979.

BUTTERFLY McQUEEN

Tragic endings seemed a pattern for screen comediennes of the era. Butterfly McQueen, best remembered as the hapless yet hilarious maid Prissy from *Gone with the Wind,* never married or had children. So the former dancer and lifelong atheist donated her remains to the Freedom of Religion Foundation upon her passing from burns sustained from a kerosene lamp malfunctioning when she tried to light it and it burst into flames.

THELMA TODD

Thelma Todd was a former Miss Massachusetts, made 120 films between 1926 and 1935, worked with Laurel and Hardy, Buster Keaton, and most famously, the Marx Brothers. She was considered beautiful, talented, and lucky. The latter ran out on December 16, 1935, when Todd was discovered dead in a garage in her still-running car, a victim of carbon monoxide poisoning. The grand jury ruled her death a suicide, but friends suspected foul play. Perhaps it was the blood and a bump on her head, plus the fact that she wasn't paying the person trying to extort her that made them feel that way.

Nobody will ever know. The body was cremated before an autopsy could be performed.

MARTHA RAYE

The Big Mouth got her name for the size of her pie hole in relation to the rest of her mug. Raye started working in vaudeville at the age of three and never stopped working. She made comedies in the '30s with the likes of Joe E. Brown, entertained troops doing USO shows during World War II, Korea, and Vietnam, had her own TV show in the '50s, appeared in *Pufnstuf* in the '70s, did commercials in the '80s, and died in the '90s after being married seven times. Her last husband tied the knot with Martha when she was seventy-five and he was forty-two. Years later, he admitted to blowing his inheritance of $3 million and being reduced to living with one of his adult daughters. That was better than what Raye's only daughter got, which was nothing. She was cut out of Raye's will due to their estrangement at the time of her death.

✳✳✳

All of these women entertained and kept Depression-era audiences laughing when the average American was fighting back tears. Through famines, foreclosures, and families in distress, comediennes became an integral part of the nation's buoyed spirits and grit. Though they didn't change the world as war waged in Europe, they helped make it a better place. Considering the price many paid for this, it's a wonder more are not mentioned more often.

MARGARET DUMONT

It's also a shame the way Margaret Dumont's name is not a household one. The Brooklyn, New York, native was trained as an operatic singer and actress. She performed on stages in Europe and the US and later as a vaudevillian in Atlantic City. At the time she was described as a "statuesque beauty" (keep in mind she was twenty years old at the time) and gained notoriety for her comedic abilities. In 1910, she married a sugar heir and retired from show business. When he died in 1918, she reluctantly returned to the Broadway stage.

Dumont did one musical comedy after another until writer George S. Kaufman pegged her play in the Marx Brothers play *The Cocoanuts* in 1925. Coming through with flying colors, she was cast in *Animal Crackers* with the brothers in 1928, then made the film *The Cocoanuts* in 1929. It was one of the first "talkies" and Margaret Dumont was now a motion-picture star. Groucho later called her the fifth Marx Brothers, and she earned the title performing with the madcap trio (or quartet when Zeppo was still on board) in seven films.

Despite the assumption that Dumont didn't understand Groucho's putdowns, the truth is she was a consummate professional and made it appear that her dowager characters were clueless. She actually found the scripts totally hilarious. This made her the most underrated comedienne of the era, and also made her death so strange in relation to her contemporaries. She died of old age. They ruled it a heart attack, but she was eighty-two years old. C'mon.

CHAPTER 4

No Apollo-gizing

"There ain't nothing an old man can do for me but bring me a message from a young one." —**Moms Mabley**

MOMS MABLEY

It's been said that comedy comes from tragedy. In that case, Jackie "Moms" Mabley must have been the funniest person alive. Born Loretta Mary Aiken, the future pioneer was raped by the town's sheriff when she was thirteen years old in her hometown of Brevard, North Carolina. It resulted in a pregnancy that went full term. Loretta had already been raped two years previously, which had also produced a child. Considering Loretta had eleven brothers and sisters, two babies was too many more mouths to feed, so midwives took both and gave them up for adoption. Her father wanted to preserve whatever reputation she had left and insisted she marry an old man.

Loretta's marriage didn't last long. The old man had a violent heart attack. Her daddy didn't linger long either. Loretta's father, a volunteer firefighter, was killed when his fire truck overturned and exploded. Momma also wasn't too lucky. On Christmas Day 1907, Loretta's mother was crossing the street when a mail truck swerved out of control and ran her over. The young girl went to live with her grandmother, a funny woman who became her inspiration and chief influence. When one of Loretta's older brothers talked to her about becoming a prostitute to help bring money into the house, it was Loretta's grandmother who told her to make something of herself instead.

Loretta, determined not to sell herself, moved to Cleveland. Her grandmother had arranged for her to live with a minister and his family. That clan put on church shows, through which Loretta learned how to sing, dance, and discovered she was funny. One day she snuck off and entered a talent contest. By observing the raw-edged comics that preceded her, the talented novice realized her material was too clean for the room and on the spot spiced up her act and got the desired response. She was hooked. Loretta returned home, packed up her things, ran away, and joined a minstrel show. She started performing for the Theatre Owners Booking Association (TOBA), circa 1915, for $14 a week, and that's where she met Jack Mabley.

Jack educated Loretta on the fine points of being a minstrel, soon after they began dating. After going to the movies and catching D. W. Griffith's *Birth of a Nation* (the cinematic classic that Griffith later admitted was created to make whites hate blacks and fear that black men had designs on white women), Loretta was determined to do art that educated black people and make them aware of the climate in which they lived. In 1918, an all-black production was released, titled *Birth of a Race,* to counter the racist D. W. Griffith epic. The movie stunk, but one of the good parts was the start of the Lincoln Motion Picture Company, incorporated in 1916; it produced black films for black people. It's mandate: "To picture the Negro as he is in his everyday life, a human being with human inclination, and one of talent and intellect."

Jack and Loretta became a couple. However, he began to take advantage of her, by taking her money for his "tutelage," as well as stealing money out of her purse. Then after one of her shows, her disapproving brother showed up. He complained about her being a stage performer (i.e., a whore). They argued and Jack butted in. Loretta had to break up the fight and told her sibling to leave, emphasizing that she's not only going to stay in show business and keep being with Jack, she's going to take his last name to boot.

The next time Loretta hit the stage, she's introduced as Jackie Mabley. The rowdy crowd is packed with couples. The year is 1920 and Jackie is curvaceous. She works the audience, which includes going down in the crowd and flirting with the men, who can't take their eyes off of her, which ticks their women off and a riot almost breaks out because of jealous dates.

Following that performance, Jack tells Jackie that she's funny but she's going to have to tone it down to keep the peace. Instead Jackie decides to make her brand of material work by altering her look. She was too young and cute to say the things she was saying, but they were the same things her grandmother used to say. That's when she realized that it's because her grandmother was old. Old people can say anything. So she modeled herself after a woman of about sixty or sixty-five wearing flappy clothes, a good woman with an eye for shady dealings. The act works and Jackie is able to say anything she wants.

Moms builds on the success at each venue and her popularity grows.

"She would sit in white men's laps, and back then you weren't even supposed to do that kind of stuff." —Edwonda White

Jack became jealous. He told her he's glad she's doing well, but he should get cut in on some of the extra money. The relationship became strained when she said no.

The troupe traveled down south, where the KKK descended on one of the theaters and set it ablaze, causing the crowd, as well as the performers, to flee. One male minstrel's was shot and barely made it back onto the bus. Another man suffered a broken arm. Jackie patched both men up, telling them mothering was something she did regularly for her brothers and sisters. She'd gained that reputation among the performers and was given the nickname "Moms." From then on, she was Jackie "Moms" Mabley. Nobody knows if Jack Mabley ever made it out of the theater, but they do know that he didn't make it onto the bus and was never heard from again.

Following a performance in Dallas, Texas, Moms got a major career break. Waiting in the wings of the theater was the vaudeville duo Butterbeans and Susie. They introduced her to the singer Ethel Waters, who they were helping, and let her know they wanted to do the same for her. The next afternoon, she went to Okeh Records and saw them rehearsing their risqué comedy song "I Want a Hot Dog for My Roll." After the session, Moms was told by the show-biz vets that she's too good for the place she was where they'd met her, and they turned her on to an agent for better bookings. She signed and began making upward of $90 a week, compared to the $14 a week she'd been pulling in with TOBA. She moved to New York City and found herself in the middle of the Harlem Renaissance.

Moms performed her comedy act in vaudeville while simultaneously auditioning for straight theater. She played venues like Connie's Inn and the Cotton Club, where she graced the stage with performers such as Louis Armstrong, Count Basie, Duke Ellington, and Cab Calloway. Moms appeared in the musical *Miss Bandana*. She gained a following in the theater community as someone to keep an eye on. Moms was eager to expand her theater credentials and sought out esteemed author Zora Neale Hurston with hopes of collaborating.

Hurston was one of the great playwrights and short story writers of the Harlem Renaissance, and Moms became entrenched in the Hurston camp. They collaborated on a play titled *Fast and Furious: A Colored Revue in 37 Scenes*. It's highly promoted and assured a long run. Besides Moms in a star-making part, the play featured a young Tim Moore, long before he portrayed Kingfish on the television version of *Amos 'n' Andy*. Unfortunately, the show was shut down by a demonstration by an anti-Hurston crowd. Moms was crushed professionally.

Personally Moms and Hurston were both black feminists, but their politics caused a bitter fight. The two close friends got into it about Booker T. Washington and the pull-yourself-up-by-the-bootstraps remedy for America's black population. Hurston rejected the black community's claims of institutionalized racism. Moms told her she's appeasing white racists and that makes her an enemy of her people. With that, the friendship ended.

Moms performed in *Blackberries of 1932* during April of that year, with Mantan Moreland and a man she would be associated with for the rest of her life, Dewey "Pigmeat" Markham. She was an extra in the early Paul Robeson picture *Emperor Jones* (1933). Robeson was huge, but was minimized for his politics. Moms enjoyed steady gigs in 1930s Harlem, including as a regular in black theater revues. Moms opened for the Duke Ellington Orchestra, Cab Calloway and his orchestra, and Count Basie's orchestra, incorporating jive talk while performing "hipster" routines about "blowing tea" and related topics into her act.

In 1939, Moms became the first female comedian to perform at Harlem's Apollo Theater, a major venue for black performers. She soon became a regular at the Apollo and would often play for fifteen-week stints, changing her act each week. Her contribution also extended to the writing of comedy shows at the Apollo, as well as writing her own act with the help of her younger brother, Eddie Parton. Her older disapproving brother brought Eddie to her and reluctantly told her that her younger brother wanted to follow in her footsteps and he wasn't going to stop him. Moms quickly became a favorite with the Apollo audiences, who began laughing as soon as she walked on the stage.

Unfortunately, haters are nothing new and Moms Mabley, being a woman, was viewed as a novelty. She'd spot white comedians in the Apollo crowd with pen and paper in hand, ripping off her material. Too bad for her haters, Moms wasn't just going to stand by and let them do it. She'd confront and admonish them from the stage. During one of these outings, a white reviewer who was present deemed Moms too cocky to review, and so her brilliance as a relevant performer went unreported to a larger mainstream audience.

The year 1939 also saw Moms participate in an ambitious jazz rendering of Shakespeare's *A Midsummer Night's Dream,* dubbed *Swingin' the Dream* and sponsored in part by the New York World's Fair. It was set in 1890s New Orleans and featured demonstrations of jazz and voodoo throughout. The remarkable cast had Louis Armstrong as Bottom, Butterfly McQueen as Puck, and Mabley as Quince. Other cast members included Dorothy, Etta and Vivian Dandridge, singer Maxine Sullivan, and dancer Norma Miller. The program stated, "Scenery based on cartoons designed by Walt Disney." The Benny Goodman Sextet and Bud Freeman's Summa Cum Laude performed compositions written by Fats Waller, W. C. Handy, Johnny Mercer, and the great Slam Stewart.

This was a project of such pedigree, Moms was bound to finally get the notice due her that so many of her fellow performers had achieved. With Eddie's help, she rehearsed diligently and knew every line backward and forward. In the end, *Swingin' the Dream* was a dismal failure. It lasted only thirteen performances—opening on November 29, 1939, and closing on December 9, at a loss of almost $100,000, an enormous sum at the time.

Moms swallowed her disappointment and kept pushing. She was featured in *Boarding House Blues,* where she played landlord to a building full of vaudeville performers behind on their rent. The writer was on the set. His name was Hal Seeger, a white man who tried to show the actors how to ham it up. Moms asked about his background, and he told her he's primarily an animator of cartoons.

Boarding House Blues also featured "Crip" Heard, a tap dancer with only one arm and one leg.

When Moms appeared on the set of her next film, Seeger was there too. He also wrote *Killer Diller* (1948). Its highlights come from Moms, who sings a song, a comedy turn from Butterfly McQueen, and a performance by the King Cole Trio. The Clark Brothers also do an amazing, high energy tap routine. The 1950s saw Moms become a popular attraction in black nightclubs around the country. However, mainstream success with white audiences still eluded her. The white press and power brokers considered an outspoken black woman not ready for prime time. Her act still dealt with her quest for a young man, but she was also more political than some cared for. Moms incorporated absurd tales from her fictive life, such as hanging out on the White House lawn with President Eisenhower, Adam Clayton Powell, Bo Diddley, and Big Maybelle.

Race-related yarns laced her act, like the story she would tell of driving in the South: "I was on my way down to Miami . . . I mean, They-ami. I was ridin' along in my Cadillac, you know, goin' through one of them little towns in South Carolina. Pass through a red light. One of them big cops come runnin' over to me, say, 'Hey, woman, don't you know you went through a red light?' I say, 'Yeah I know I went through a red light.' 'Well, what did you do that for?' I said, "Cause I seen all you white folks goin' on the green light . . . I thought the red light was for us!'"

While peers like Mantan Moreland and Pigmeat Markham achieved success on film, Moms was relegated to extra work in low-budget barely seen films. She was doing fine onstage, but she remained an underground phenomenon, not in demand by the coveted mainstream audience. Then in 1956 Vanguard Records released *A Night at the Apollo*. The album's a fascinating social document with liner notes written by former indirect adversary Langston Hughes (he had a public beef with her one-time friend Zora Neale Hurston). Comedian George Kirby, best known for his famous impression of Pearl Bailey, also performed. There's an elongated "amateur competition" hosted by house MC Leonard Reed with teenage vocalists competing for the top prize. (Reed was a lauded vaudeville tap dancer who invented the famed steps of the Shim Sham Shimmy—his vaudeville dance act was billed as "Brains as Well as Feet.") Vocalists Danny Rogers and Pearl Jones performed, as did a woman named Doreen Vaughn, who was partially booed by the notoriously cruel Apollo patrons. Doo-woppers the Heartbreakers and the Keynoters received generous ovations.

In 1960, Moms was approached by Chess Records. She was reluctant to jump labels. But they wined and dined her and did several elaborate stunts to get her attention and trust. Finally she entered the Chess Records offices in Chicago. The walls were adorned with pictures of Muddy Waters, Howlin' Wolf, Little Walter, Sonny Boy Williamson, Memphis Slim, Bo Diddley, Yusef Lateef, and Chuck Berry. They have a signing ceremony complete with champagne. *Moms Mabley: The Funniest Woman Alive* is recorded live at Chicago's Tivoli Theatre and the record earned Moms a gold record. Chess then immediately recorded *Moms Mabley at the "UN"* at the Uptown Theatre in Philadelphia.

Based on her album's success, Moms gained an elite following, including *Playboy* magazine founder Hugh Hefner. He called her in for a personal meeting and outlined a strategy for an album he wanted her to record at his Playboy club. *Moms Mabley at the Playboy Club* has a totally different sound than her previous two albums. Only a small smattering of applause greets her introduction. It's an all-white audience. Moms wanted the crossover, but on her terms. The church bombings, the fire hoses, the lunch counter sit-ins, and the freedom marches were occurring frequently, and the intensity of the civil rights struggle was heating up, and Moms wanted white audiences to hear her message now. Leonard Chess bought a full-page ad in *Billboard* announcing her next album release.

Moms was political onstage, but was confronted by the Negro press about her lack of personal commitment.

She stepped it up. Martin Luther King Jr.'s joined by many celebrities on his marches, including Dick Gregory, Charlton Heston and a fully invested Moms. Few take notice of her presence because she doesn't wear her famous stage attire; she walks along with the freedom marchers dressed in regular street clothes and without the Moms Mabley persona. It's Loretta Aiken marching for what's right

After her performance at Carnegie Hall, Chess Records lost Moms Mabley to the far whiter Mercury Records. Moms's *The Word* and *Out on a Limb* are released. In 1965, she has a high-profile cameo in the Steve McQueen vehicle *The Cincinnati Kid* playing a blues singer.

Chess Records re-issued their Moms Mabley albums. Since white people were getting hip to her, they had no intention of not making those dollars. Moms wasn't happy with it, but there was nothing she could do. Most of the repackaged works featured her and Pigmeat since they didn't have enough old Moms material to go around. One of the albums they put out was called *Moms Mabley—The Men in My Life*. It was an interesting title and opened up a can of worms.

Moms had cultivated a reputation as a lover of younger men, but not since the days of Jack Mabley had she been linked to any particular man. The press took notice and several articles were written implying Moms was a closet lesbian. She personally found it funny to be mentioned in the same breath with glamorous Hollywood celebrities like Claudette Colbert and Marlene Dietrich. When asked about it by her brother Eddie before a show, she simply replied, "If I was white, they'd know for sure. They're just saying that because men are too scared to be good groupies."

In the mid-60s, her albums were purchased by both blacks and whites. However, both cultures experienced the adventure of buying Moms. Due to the adult nature of the recordings, patrons would go to the record store, have their Moms Mabley record handed to them wrapped in brown paper, pay discreetly, and exit.

She never stopped trying to advance her standing in

show business despite the obvious obstacles and resistance. Moms attended a multi-network convention. A panel of TV executives addressed current trends in television. Moms stood up and asked how is it she was so popular on the streets but couldn't get onto a TV sound stage. An exec wasted no time in telling her that she was too raunchy for television audiences. He cited the places she performed as reason to keep her kind of performer locked out. Moms response was quick and received a standing ovation. "It's you and others in your position who keep me working where I have to use that kind of material." She threw down a challenge that she could conform to television standards like any seasoned professional if only given the chance.

A Time for Laughter: A Look at Negro Humor in America was a special produced by Harry Belafonte and part of an hour-long variety series called *ABC Stage 67*. The program showcased the greatest African American comedians performing new sketches written especially for the program. Godfrey Cambridge and Diana Sands played a couple that gets on the nerves of their maid, Moms, when they try to act like white people. The show also featured Dick Gregory, playing a civil rights marcher in a prison cell, delivering a funny monologue about black power. Pigmeat Markham played a judge in a sketch in which he presided over Harry Belafonte and Diahann Carroll as a quarreling couple. Richard Pryor delivered a solo piece as an undertaker who has to deliver an awkward eulogy after the clergyman failed to appear. George Kirby played all seven characters in one sketch, and Redd Foxx delivered a routine as a pool hustler ranting about racial inequality.

The program was nominated for an Emmy for that year's Outstanding Variety Program. Moms and her friends watched eagerly on TV as it lost to a Bob Hope special. Her response was pointed as usual. "Maybe I ought to go entertain some troops from five miles from the front lines. We'd have won too if we had Ann-Margaret influencing the judges."

No matter—she got a job working on *The Smothers*

Brothers Comedy Hour. She performed her stand-up act for four minutes, joked about the "racial situation," and made CBS executives nervous. The staff was told not to alert Moms to the fan mail and number of fan calls she received from the counterculture kids who were rapidly becoming Moms Mabley converts. CBS invited her back due to Moms obvious popularity, but behaved as though they're the ones doing her a favor.

The week before Christmas she did *The Merv Griffin Show,* sharing the panel with fellow stand-up comedian Jack Carter and former boxer Rocky Graziano. She destroyed; everybody was in stitches. Moms returned to Merv's show an unprecedented ten days after her previous appearance, so popular was her first guest shot. Once again TV executives minimized the rapid return by saying another minor performer had to cancel and would she be gracious enough fill in.

Her agent fought for films, but nobody gave her a shot. It was the beginning of the Blaxploitation era, but unless Moms was willing to play Shaft's mother, there was no way they could picture her in those types of movies. So she plodded along in TV doing *The Flip Wilson Show, The Pearl Bailey Show, Laugh-In, Music Scene, The Tonight Show with Johnny Carson,* and guest starred on the mild-mannered sitcom known as *The Bill Cosby Show.* Mabley played Cosby's elderly aunt who shows up unannounced for a visit while Bill is busy putting the moves on a girl. Mabley's husband and Cosby's uncle was portrayed by Mantan Moreland. Over the course of the episode, Mabley and Moreland fight and bicker, driving Cosby up the wall until he has to act.

Moms was preparing an anti-war routine for her next appearance on the *Smothers Brothers Comedy Hour,* but the show was abruptly canceled. Free speech on TV was taking a hit, but her records were still selling. She was a bona fide star. Her salary at the Apollo increased from $1,000 a week in 1961 to a $10,000 a week as a headliner in 1968. After nearly fifty years in show business, Moms was an overnight success.

Following the disappointment of the lost *Smothers*

Brothers opportunity, Moms was driven to use her newfound stardom to speak out against the war, and nobody had a greater following than her old friend Reverend King. She contacted him and requested a joint venture where she could speak with him on the ills of racism and the war. He embraced her idea and informed her that they should iron out the details once he returned from an appearance he's was about to make for the striking garbage workers in Tennessee. When Moms received word that King was assassinated, she was inconsolable.

In 1969, Mercury had its greatest success with Moms when she covered Dion's "Abraham, Martin & John," a sentimental piece of pop that paid homage to Abraham Lincoln, Martin Luther King Jr., JFK, and his slain brother, Bobby. The original made it to number four on the charts, and Moms's interpretation also broke into *Billboard*'s top 40. At seventy-five years of age, Moms Mabley became the oldest person ever to have a Top 40 hit in the US. That same year Hugh Hefner booked Moms for his television series *Playboy After Dark*. She appeared on *The Mike Douglas Show,* performing and sitting down with Ralph Nader; *The Merv Griffin Show,* where she sat on a panel with Woody Allen, and she did a killer set on *The Ed Sullivan Show.*

Moms shot *Its Your Thing,* a concert film featuring the Isley Brothers, the Eddie Hawkins Singers, and Ike and Tina Turner. Unfortunately, Moms new label, Stax, became a bit too ambitious, essentially going bankrupt with several ill-conceived ideas; one plan was a new subsidiary devoted to comedy albums, Partee Records. Moms would have her last vinyl release put out by the division. The Mabley LP was titled *I Like Them Young* and was released in 1972. It featured Stax session players and former members of Booker T. and the MGs, Duck Dunn and Al Jackson, backing her up throughout.

She was a presenter at the 1973 Grammy Awards. She tore the house down, leaving young executives who took notice to ask, "Why isn't this woman in movies?" and received no satisfying answers. So soon after, she was making *Amazing Grace,* her starring comedy role in 1974 and her last major project. On May 23, 1975, the living legend took her own journey home from White Plains, New York, when Moms Mabley died after a fatal heart attack. Comedians of all races credit her as an inspiration. Over the course of her lengthy career, she recorded twenty albums and she's remembered fondly by fans and historians, but to the public she's more of a reference. Few can recite a Mabley joke or imitate her character. The same can't be said about Lucy, Aunt Esther, or Granny Clampett. The difference being the new medium Moms hardly got to take advantage of in her heyday. She was in the era of television, but not a creature of it. A *Mom's Mabley Show* could've been an innovative TV show and preserver of a true comedy icon. Well, at least we have the few recorded treasures we do and the many artists whom the tube embraced.

CHAPTER 5

Get the Ball Rolling

"I'd rather regret the things I've done than regret the things I haven't done." —**Lucille Ball**

Nostalgia forces the best memories from our subconscious. The reality is that a glance at a *TV Guide* from the '50s could be used as a sleep aid as opposed to a glimpse at the golden era. There were programs like *Ozark Jubilee, The Dotty Mack Show* (where from 1953 to 1956, actress Dotty Mack would lip-synch and dance to popular songs of the '50s), and the ironically named *Coke Time with Eddie Fisher*. It would also be considered light reading because there was barely anything on. Keep in mind this was at a time when television went *off*. At 2 a.m. the screen went black and there was nothing you could do about it. Nothing except sit there, listen to the national anthem, and watch that Indian head logo until the high whistle tone lulled you to sleep.

Thank God reruns were invented. A lot of good stuff from this period didn't make it, and thankfully most of the experimental dredge didn't either. But because of reruns, for as long as most people can remember, Lucille Ball has always been on television. It was programs like *The Honeymooners, The Milton Berle Show,* and *I Love Lucy* that helped popularize the fledgling medium and allowed it to give theatrical movies a run for their money and close down many major movie theaters. In the 1950s, TV was the new thing and Lucy was its first queen. It was a long route to the throne.

LUCILLE BALL

L ucille Desiree Ball was born in Jamestown, New York, on August 6, 1911, and immediately started losing things. Since her father, Fred, was a linesman, they moved so much she'd always lose houses and friends. While her mother was pregnant with Lucy's brother, Frederick, she lost her father to typhoid fever in 1915. Years later, while living with her grandparents, the house and furnishings were lost to a court judgment after a local boy was shot by someone on the property under her grandfather's supervision. Seems the only thing Lucy found during her sad childhood was her niche. Her stepfather was a Shriner and Lucy got her first taste of stage life as a twelve-year-old chorus girl.

Despite a shining moment of self-realization, Lucy's pattern of loss continued. At fourteen, she found herself without her twenty-one-year-old thug boyfriend, Johnny DeVita, after her mother, DeeDee shipped her off to the John Murray Anderson School of Dramatic Arts in New York City. It was a move to remove her from a bad influence, but that didn't help much when her drama coaches told her she "had no future at all as a performer" and she returned home with her tail between her legs. Lucy went back to New York two years later and started booking jobs as a fashion model, and then caught an unknown illness and lost two years recovering. In 1932, she returned and worked as a Chesterfield cigarette girl, and on the Broadway chorus line under the name Diane Belmont. Under any name the losses kept stacking up. She lost her gig working for Earl Carroll and his Vanities. She was fired from *Rio Rita* by Flo Ziegfeld. She even got canned by the Shubert brothers.

Lucille Ball got tired of losing work that was just work to get by and became a full-time actress. RKO Pictures signed her as a contract player, and she appeared in shorts and films with the Three Stooges, the Marx Brothers, and many times with Fred Astaire and Ginger Rogers. She cranked out enough low-budget quickie flicks that Hollywood insiders labeled her "Queen of the Bs". Her response was to expand into radio for the exposure (as well as some needed additional income). It was while working in radio that Lucy met Gail Gordon, who would become a longtime friend and colleague.

The 1940s saw a pronounced change in Lucy's personal and professional life. She met the bandleader Desi Arnaz in 1940 when they worked together in Rodgers and Hart's *Too Many Girls*. It was an odd meeting. In the morning he didn't care much for the brunette, but when Desi saw her later that same day, they were the best of friends. They were so chummy, they eloped the following year and the year after that Desi was drafted into the US Army. He had a knee injury, which kept him in Los Angeles. So the military had him booking USO shows to boost the morale of wounded soldiers returning home. Lucy worked in the film *DuBarry Was a Lady* and dyed her hair red for the part. It became her signature style, but the loss of brunette locks apparently made her lose a little patience. She and Desi had been having a rocky go of it, with plenty going against them, especially during that era. She was Scottish/French/Irish and English. He was Cuban. She was six years older than him, causing them each to lie about their ages (up three for him, down for her) for social acceptance, and they were both working all the time, but not with each other. In 1944, she'd had enough and filed for a divorce. Later that same year, she reconciled with Desi and withdrew the divorce.

The Band-Aid was on the severed limb, but the Desi Arnazes needed surgery. Relief came in the form of a radio show Lucy was signed to in 1948. It was called *My Favorite Husband* and was such a success that CBS wanted Lucy to adapt it for television. She agreed as long as Desi was the favorite husband and their production company, Desilu, produced it. The network hated that idea. Or at least the notion that a redhead would be romantically involved (married or not) to a Latin lover on a comedy show. So a pilot was shot and the network said it sucked. Well, Lucy wasn't going to lose this battle, and took the production on tour playing their show to live audiences, tweaking it along the way and making it a smash hit on the road. The network changed its mind, and in 1951 *I Love Lucy* was scheduled to make its debut.

However, prior to their now historic drop date, some details had to be ironed out. Lucy and Desi lived on the West Coast. Live prime-time TV was shot on the East Coast on cheap-looking kinescope and shown to West Coast people three hours later. So either Lucy and Desi would have to relocate to New York (which they had no intention of doing) or the show would have to be aired for East Coasters the following day (since it would be too late to broadcast three hours after West Coast airings, and executives certainly weren't going for that). The solution came in an offer Desilu made to the sponsor Phillip Morris: they'd take a pay cut, film the show themselves, and retain the rights. That way they would foot the bill for processing and the show could be aired to all the same evening. Since nobody knew what a rerun was and most executives thought audiences had no appetite to see a show twice, CBS took the bait and the rights to *I Love Lucy* reverted back to Desilu after the initial airing, making Desilu untold millions in the lucrative syndication market.

Now that the pesky business aspects were out of the way, it was time to make the series. In front of the camera, *I Love Lucy* presented the couple as an up-and-coming bandleader/club owner with a wacky wife always trying to get into his shows. It also featured Desi's choices of Vivian Vance and William Frawley (Ball wanted Bea Benederet and Gale Gordon) as their landlords, Ethel and Fred Mertz. Behind the camera, the stars were the producers, Jess Oppenheimer and Arnaz, the excellent writing staff headed by Madelyn Pugh Davis and Bob Carroll Jr., and cameraman Karl Freund, who'd shot the original 1931 version of *Dracula* with Bela Lugosi and directed 1932's *The Mummy* with Boris Karloff. For *I*

Love Lucy, he developed flat lighting so shots didn't have to be constantly relit, as well as his three-camera innovation for live-audience filming. Long shots, medium shots, close-ups—everything taken for granted by modern sitcom viewers were refined for the medium by Freund and the Desilu staff of technicians.

To date *I Love Lucy* has been on the air for over sixty years. As you read this, somewhere somebody is watching an episode. The show was such a smash, her pregnancy and delivery were televised. Every Hollywood star wanted to make a guest appearance, and many did: Bob Hope, William Holden, John Wayne, Hedda Hopper, Rock Hudson, Robert Taylor, Eve Arden, Van Johnson, Cornel Wilde, Harpo Marx, Richard Widmark, Charles Boyer, Orson Welles, Jimmy Demaret, Tennessee Ernie Ford, Claude Akins, Rudy Vallee, Tallulah Bankhead, Fred MacMurray, June Haver, Betty Grable, Harry James, Fernando Lamas, Maurice Chevalier, Danny Thomas, Red Skelton, Paul Douglas, Howard Duff, Ida Lupino, Milton Berle, Bob Cummings, Ernie Kovacs, Edie Adams, and Superman. Calling it a cultural milestone is far from hyperbole. Besides, the story lines of hilarious episodes have been repeated countless times over the decades by lesser sitcoms, entire books have been written about the show, and courses about *I Love Lucy* and its place in television lore are taught.

I Love Lucy also advanced the cause of women and comediennes in particular. Lucille Ball was the first woman in television to head a production company. Desilu held sway over TV programming for the next decade with hits like *Our Miss Brooks, Make Room for Daddy, The Untouchables, Mission: Impossible, Star Trek, My Three Sons, The Andy Griffith Show, The Dick Van Dyke Show,* and *I Spy.* The company was a behemoth that kept devouring no matter the drama behind the scenes. When the marriage with Desi didn't work out, Ball bought out his share and became a hands-on studio head until 1967; at that time, Desilu merged with Paramount Pictures.

In the meanwhile, Lucy was on top. *I Love Lucy* made her a star in her own lane. Regarding her own show, though, Lucy admitted she was a brave actress, but not a natural comedienne. She was terrible at table reads each and every week. It was excruciating, but she would go home with the script and work it. The next day, Lucille Ball was Lucy, not missing one hilarious beat. She had to stave off loss. She and Desi had suffered through three miscarriages (in 1942, 1949, and 1950) throughout the course of their union, and they'd finally been blessed with Lucie Desiree Arnaz on July 17, 1951, three months shy of the show's premiere. The birth of Desiderio Alberto Arnaz IV (aka Little Ricky) in 1953 made the cover of *TV Guide* that January (it was a planned cesarean). If she made it through the miracle of child birth, she could definitely pull off a sitcom. She was on a roll.

Then the wolves came knocking at her door and threatened to reintroduce the long-stagnant sense of loss back into her life. A registered Communist in 1936, Ball was hauled in front of William A. Wheeler of the House Un-American Committee on September 4, 1953, to answer charges. Despite testimony to the contrary over a decade before, Lucy stated that she registered only to appease her grandfather. She never had any intent or ever voted for any Communist Party candidate. The press was on the attack until a statement by FBI director J. Edgar Hoover put the matter to rest when he said *I Love Lucy* was his favorite TV program. On the next taping, the issue was further put to rest when Desi said, "The only thing red about Lucy is her hair, and even that's not legitimate," to an audience's thunderous applause. In the public's eyes, Ball was no commie, just a slightly naïve granddaughter.

The public also viewed Lucy as a caring, loving mother and happily married wife. They were wrong on both counts. Her daughter, Lucie, later told of Lucy's controlling nature and tendency to interfere in the personal lives of her offspring. That was in her future. In Lucy's present, and she and Desi were in a strained relationship at best. He was drinking heavily and she was busy being busy. Running the rapidly expanding and thoroughly demanding Desilu was also taking its toll. On May 4, 1960, Lucy and Desi divorced. It was a mere two months after filming their last episode together.

The next year Lucy was on Broadway in the musical production of *Wildcats*. Her friend and fellow actress Paula Stewart introduced her to a comic thirteen years her junior named Gary Morton. She married Morton, and her next show was *The Lucy Show* pairing her again with Vivian Vance. This time Lucy's character was single and working at a bank. Gale Gordon played her boss, Mr. Mooney. Two other shows followed. The successful *Here's Lucy* in the late '60s and the ill-fated *Life with Lucy* in 1986. The cancelation after two months of the latter sent Lucy into a depression and caused her to withdraw. On April 18, 1989, she complained of chest pains and was rushed to Cedar Sinai, where she required emergency surgery. The aorta of a twenty-seven-year-old was placed into the seventy-seven-year-old Ball, and for a while it worked. It was the rupture of a second aortic valve that sent her into a state of unconsciousness from which she never recovered. Lucy died on April 26, 1989. Her reruns never will.

VIVIAN VANCE

It's a downright sacrilege to discuss the professional success of Lucile Ball without devoting words to her selfless sidekick, Vivian Vance. Born Vivian Jones, this Kansas native was too rebellious to conform to her mother's strict religious beliefs and moved to Albuquerque, New Mexico, where she founded a local theater, appeared in many of the plays, and then made her way to New York for some serious study.

Vance was primarily a chorus girl on Broadway. It was 1932. By the '50s she'd gotten roles in highly regarded productions, receiving strong notices but nothing to write home about. So she didn't. She did want to tell the folks back in KC about her new job as Ethel Mertz when Desi Arnaz chose her for the role. Then again the television set would do that for her, starting in 1951 and ending in 1977 when she made her last appearance alongside Lucille Ball. Oddly enough Lucy didn't want Vivian Vance at first. She had envisioned an older, less attractive actress for Ethel Mertz. To compensate, the producers dressed Vance in frumpy clothes. Eventually Lucy warmed up to Vance and respected her talents. So despite a rocky start, the duo shared life on three sitcoms (*I Love Lucy, The Lucy Show,* and four guest-starring episodes on *Here's Lucy*).

Individually Vance became known as the best second banana in television history and the first winner of an Emmy for Outstanding Supporting Actress.

Vance didn't achieve such adulation and success without hitting some bumps along the way. She endured feuds with William Frawley (she referred to the Fred Mertz actor, who was twenty-two years her senior, as "the stubborn-headed little Irishman"). The bad blood didn't get any better in 1957 when Desi Arnaz wanted to do a spin-off for the Mertzes, but Vance refused because she didn't want to work one on one with Frawley, who had jumped at the idea. She wanted her own show. Arnaz financed the pilot, but CBS rejected it, so she remained Ethel Mertz in the retooled versions of *I Love Lucy*. Arnaz morphed the half-hour show into *The Lucille Ball–Desi Arnaz Show, The Lucy-Desi Comedy Hour,* and *The Lucy-Desi Show*.

Once the *Lucy* bonanza ended, Vance made several made-for-TV films, became a spokesperson for Maxwell House coffee, and did a handful of reunion shows with Ball. Vance was married four times, but none of the unions produced children. It was said that her third husband, Philip Ober, physically abused her, and it wasn't until 1961 that she found happiness with her fourth husband, literary agent John Dodds. They remained together until her death on August 17, 1979, of bone cancer.

AUDREY MEADOWS

Besides *I Love Lucy,* one of the few highlights from this boring age was *The Honeymooners,* starring Jackie Gleason, Art Carney, Joyce Randolph, and underrated yet incomparable Audrey Meadows. What makes her accomplishments so incredible is she held her own with Gleason. Here's a man who hated to rehearse, so most of the lines thrown at Meadows on *live* television were being done so for the very first time and she never dropped a single one.

Nothing in anybody's background could prepare them for working with a force of nature like Gleason, especially Meadows. She was born in China to Episcopalian missionary parents. When she returned home to the States, she became a singer on Broadway and comic relief on radio before she got the part of Alice Kramden (by default, when original actress Pert Kelton was blacklisted). Initially the Great One thought Meadows too classy to play the poor housewife, that is until Audrey submitted a picture of her looking more like the Alice Kramden in his head and got the part. Once that was settled, the next question was: How's this religious mike jockey going to keep up with Jackie? She not only kept up with Gleason, she was often ahead of him. In the real world, she's the only one of the cast who got royalties when the show went into syndication. So Meadows was not only a great improvisational comedienne—she also sure knew how to pick a lawyer. Meadows also knew how to pick a husband, the second time around anyway. In 1961, she married the president of Continental Airlines in Honolulu, Hawaii—Robert Six. Audrey became an advisory director of Continental Airlines and served as director of the First National Bank in Denver for eleven years; she was the first woman to hold the position. When Bob Six died in 1986, she continued her work for Continental. In 1995, her tenure was cut short when she was diagnosed with lung cancer and given a year to live. Audrey Meadows died on February 3, 1996.

IMOGENE COCA

While Lucy was trying to get into every show at Ricky's club and the Kramdens were bickering about everything, Imogene Coca was mugging it up on *Your Show of Shows*. Starting her career as a child acrobat in vaudeville, she studied ballet and had hoped for a life as a serious artist. Ha! In her forties, she woke up and became a seriously funny comedienne with a rubber face, impeccable timing, and all. Coca not only appeared in the classics with Sid Caesar, she won a Best Actress Emmy in '51 and got her own show, which ran in '55 and '56.

Coca worked as a comedienne her entire career. From 1963 to 1964, she played a comic's assistant in the NBC sitcom *Grindl,* and from 1966 to 1967, she played a cavewoman with Joe E. Ross in *It's About Time..* She guest starred on everybody's sitcom, variety show, and special from the '50s to the '80s. Coca did cabaret, theater, television, movies, and voiced cartoons. Married twice, she had no children. She did, however, leave a line of influenced comediennes such as Lily Tomlin, Tracy Ullman, and Whoopi Goldberg when she passed away on June 2, 2001, of natural causes tied into Alzheimer's disease.

NANETTE FABRAY

When powerhouse Imogene Coca left Sid Caesar and company, there was a huge gaping hole to be filled. Nanette Fabray came ready to work. By the time the former Tony Award winner and quadruple threat was done, Fabray was a household name and recipient of three Emmy Awards. She'd been preparing to shine. A performer as a child, one of Nanette's tap-dancing teachers was Bill "Bojangles" Robinson. She made her first stage appearance at age three and her film debut when she was four in an *Our Gang* short as an extra. Fabray did vaudeville productions, singing and dancing, and was soon gaining recognition as a musical comedy and theater star. *Caesar's Hour* ('54–'56) was a culmination of her work and exposure, but it ended because of a blunder. Fabray's manager made demands unknown to Fabray in exchange for her to do another season of the show. She and Sid Caesar didn't unravel the situation until years later and buried the hatchet.

PAT CARROLL

All misunderstandings aside, Sid Caesar knew how to pick his comediennes. When Pat Carroll won an Emmy for *Caesar's Hour* in 1956, it was icing on a big comedienne's cake of winners. Born in Shreveport, Louisiana, in 1927, Pat Carroll was a regular on the Danny Thomas sitcom, *Make Room for Daddy*. She played Shirley's mother on *Laverne and Shirley*, appeared on countless game shows, and did the voice of Ursula in *The Little Mermaid* film and TV series.

✳✳✳

Besides Pat Carroll, the '50s saw other notables on television, such as Eve Arden, whose hilarious portrayal of English teacher Connie Brooks, the teacher every teacher wanted to be, on *Our Miss Brooks* (on radio and television) earned her real teaching offers and various awards from teaching organizations from around the country. Ann B. Davis, an Emmy Award winner for playing Schultzy on *The Bob Cummings Show*. French-born Jean Carroll, who made over twenty appearances on *The Ed Sullivan Show* and had her own self-titled sitcom from 1953 to 1954. Mary Wickes guest starred all over the place, from *I Love Lucy*, *The Lucy Show*, *Make Room for Daddy*, *Dennis the Menace*, and *Here's Lucy* to films with Abbott and Costello. Wickes's 5' 10" gangly frame was omnipresent. Betty Walker also deserves recognition for her five comedy albums, numerous television appearances, and brief film career. Her claim to fame was her telephone act, where she yakked it up with her unseen friend "Ceil" on the other line. In film, Ann Sothern had found success as Maisie, the burlesque dancer involved in comedy intrigue, and got the movie series spun off into a popular radio show, *The Adventures of Maisie,* in the late '40s. On the more prestigious side, Judy Holiday won an Oscar as Best Actress for her role as the scatter-brained Billie Dawn in *Born Yesterday*.

However, stand-up comedy stages were another matter. It wasn't that women weren't working in comedy. It was that women in comedy in this era received little notice if the image of that woman was not coming out of a glowing box. Outside of Moms Mabley, the showbiz landscape for women on stage was virtually barren. A rare exception was Pearl Williams.

PEARL WILLIAMS

The self-taught pianist became the accompanist for the Louis Prima Band the same night she auditioned, in 1938. Fourteen years later, she got her comedy calling when a heckler drove her to say, "Oh, fuck off," and her new career was born. Williams became a foul-mouth hit. She recorded nine "party albums" and credited her chief influence as Sophie Tucker, who told Williams upon meeting her that "You're me at your age, only better." After forty-six years in show business, Williams retired in Florida and died of heart disease in 1991 at the age of seventy-seven.

BELLE BARTH

Another Tucker disciple was Belle Barth, known in some circles as the female Lenny Bruce. In 1953, she was arrested and fined $25. After a series of such cases, Belle was hit with a $1.6 million lawsuit for allegedly corrupting the morals of two schoolteachers who attended one of her shows. We don't know what they expected to learn at the performance of a dirty comedienne, but we do know they didn't get the money because the judge threw their case out, sighting their the claim that Belle's words harmed their health to be unfounded. Like Pearl Williams, Belle recorded nine adult party albums and called Miami Beach, Florida, home, where she also opened her own pub. She was married five times (twice to the same man) and died at the age of fifty-nine in 1971 after becoming ill in Las Vegas in 1970.

RUSTY WARREN

Ilene Goldman, aka Rusty Warren, was adopted by a New England couple at six months old and studied music under future Boston Pops conductor Arthur Fiedler. An accomplished pianist, Warren recorded for Jubilee Records and began her comedy career in the early 1950s. It wasn't long before she became known as the mother of the sexual revolution, talking about sex from a female point of view at a time when sex wasn't talked about at all, not publicly onstage anyway and certainly not by women.

Rusty Warren recorded fifteen comedy albums. Her most famous was called *Knockers Up*. It was a call for the women in her audience to parade around the showroom with their knockers held high. She also had a risqué song, which asked the ladies to remove their bras and be free. It was titled "Bounce Your Boobies." She was hidden from the mainstream, but she was a heroine on the underground circuit. Considered ahead of her time sexually, times caught up with Rusty Warren in the mid-'60s when the real sexual revolution kicked in and her brand of naughty was deemed merely nice. Female comedy and the perception of women was about to go through a drastic change.

CHAPTER 6

Times Were a-Changin'

"I've been on a diet for two weeks and all I've lost is two weeks"
—**Totie Fields**

The late '50s saw women in a different light. Rosa Parks lit the fuse of the civil rights movement by being civilly disobedient and remaining seated where she sat. The safe sounds of Patti Page and Doris Day were replaced by male rock-'n'-roll screamers and it was the ladies who fueled their ascension. Sex appeal went even further when the nation transferred power from an old golf-loving war-general president in Eisenhower to a strapping young playboy war hero in John F. Kennedy. Women became a coveted voting block for Camelot's ruler.

By the 1960s, television was making huge strides for women as well. There were more shows to watch and trends had developed. Westerns and doctor shows were on every channel along with the news, some sports, and, of course, comedies. In that area, rural comedies were queen. Irene Ryan was a hoot as cantankerous Granny Clampett on *The Beverly Hillbillies,* along with Donna Douglas as the busting-at-the-seams Ellie Mae. City-loving Eva Gabor constantly one-upped exasperated country-convert husband Eddie Albert on *Green*

Acres, and nobody made 'em bust a gut better than Minnie Pearl on *Hee Haw.*

Girlfriends with shows named after them also pulled in steady ratings. *Gidget,* starring Sally Fields, was a tour de force for the actress, but her character only wanted the beach and boys. Few would've predicted *The Flying Nun,* Burt Reynolds, and two Oscars in her future. *The Patty Duke Show* saw Patty too preoccupied with Patty (and often her twin cousin, Cathy) to keep a boyfriend. On the other hand, Danny's daughter, Marlo Thomas, was *That Girl,* the perfect beau if you liked them obedient, whiny, and clueless, which Ted Bessell obviously did. Then there was the ultimate male fantasy—*I Dream of Jeannie.* Have her come in and out of a bottle depending on whether you wanted her around or not. To her credit, Barbara Eden pulled it off naval and all, while another Barbara—Feldon—was comedic spy Agent 99 in *Get Smart.*

Honorable mention to Agnes Morehead's portrayal of Endora (*Bewitched*), who made viewers laugh at a true mother-in-law slam—she was a real witch who blatantly hated her son-in-law and turned him into everything but to her liking.

Marion Lorne (Aunt Clara on *Bewitched*) kept viewers in stitches with her forgetfulness and botched spells. She was so beloved the producers didn't even attempt to replace her character after Lorne's untimely death due to a heart attack in the fifth season; she instead received a posthumous Emmy for Best Supporting Actress.

Kaye Ballard was the other half of *The Mother-in-Laws* (Eve Arden was the other mother). Ballard, a musical-revue-seasoned comedienne, became the decade's number-one female sidekick with her turn on *The Doris Day Show.*

Alice Ghostley was the queen of recurring characters. From Esmeralda, the shy witch on *Bewitched*, and cousin Alice on *Mayberry RFD* to a small-apartment roommate on *The Julie Andrew's Hour*, Perky Sugarbaker's friend on *Designing Women,* and Irna Wallingsford on *Evening Shade,* Ghostley's was the face TV viewers got used to seeing.

Ventriloquism was even covered by Shari Lewis. Since the early 1950s, she'd been educating and entertaining with her puppets, Hush Puppy, Charlie Horse, and, her most popular, Lamp Chop on New York television. In 1960, NBC gave Lewis her first network show, and generations grew up on her wit until the twelve-time Emmy winner passed in 1998.

Women were all over the landscape in various sizes, temperaments, and ages. The beauty of comedy is that you can do it as long as you want or as long as it will let you.

PHYLLIS DILLER

P hyllis Diller was born on July 17, 1917, became a comedienne in 1952, and retired in 2005. During that fifty-three-year career, she embedded herself in our conscious. Her laugh, hair, and cigarette holder are all trademarks. Most comics are lucky to have one. Oh, and did I mention her signature muumuus?

Phyllis Diller. Most of us can't recall when we didn't know her name. Like most stalwart entertainers, she was more than just a one-note player. Phyllis Diller was a comedienne, actress, musician, painter, voice-over artist, and author. She was synonymous with madcap and wacky. She began a life in front of the camera on the show *Phyllis Dillis, the Homely Friendmaker*. The series of episodes ran only fifteen minutes, but Diller had more than that amount of fame to live.

She got her big comedy break in 1955. Diller appeared at the Purple Onion. She played the renowned club for eighty-seven straight weeks. From there she was on the very popular *Del Courtney's Showcase* on local television in the Bay Area and got connected to Bob Hope. Old Ski Nose proved to be a valuable career boost. Diller did twenty-three of his specials, three movies, and toured with him in Vietnam for the USO.

Diller was a busy entertainer in the '60s. Besides the three Bob Hope films (with *Boy, Did I Get a Wrong Number* being the only box office success), Diller also showed up in over a dozen other usually low-budget films, exceptions being 1961's

Splendor in the Grass and the 1967 animated feature length with Boris Karloff, titled *Mad Monster Party.* She starred in two television comedies: *The Pruitts of Southampton* on ABC from '66 to '67, and her own variety show, *The Beautiful Phyllis Diller Show,* for network rival NBC in 1968. In 1969, she was a replacement for Carol Channing on Broadway in *Hello Dolly.* She recorded a half dozen comedy LPs, and never being one to take herself too seriously, made frequent appearances on *Rowan & Martin's Laugh-In,* where she'd do bits like running behind a garbage truck and ask, "Am I too late?" only to be told by the driver "No, jump right in."

Phyllis Diller's distinctive voice served her well throughout her career. She's played herself on more than one occasion, 1972's *The New Scooby-Doo Movies* being the most notable. She's also lent her vocals to Pixar's *It's a Bug's Life* (1998), *The Adventures of Jimmy Neutron: Boy Genius* (2002), and in a recurring role as Peter Griffin's mother, Thelma, in *Family Guy* (2006).

The woman had fifteen different plastic surgery procedures. The work on her was so successful her surgeons won awards. She also once posed for *Playboy* magazine. Once was apparently enough since the photos were never used.

A lifelong nonsmoker (the cigarette holders were mere stage props) and twice married, Diller outlived most of her children. Out of the six, one died of cancer, another of a stroke, another lived for only two weeks in an incubator, and one suffered from schizophrenia most of her life. The other two children lived relatively healthy lives. Diller herself suffered a heart attack in 1999, and a bad fall in 2005 forced her to be fitted with a pacemaker and also forced her to retire from active show business. She kept busy making occasional guest TV appearances and collecting myriad of awards over the years until her death on August 20, 2012 at age 95.

TOTIE FIELDS

To her shopping center owner dad, Sophie Feldman was a nice Jewish girl born in Hartford, Connecticut, in 1930.

She became the hilarious and multitalented Totie Fields later
on. Well, not too much later. She started out singing at local
radio stations by the time she was four years old, toured the
Borscht Belt at fourteen, and before she was twenty worked
as a tummler (a job normally reserved for men) in Boston-
area strip clubs. The gig consisted of hosting in between the
strippers. It was around this time that she adopted the name
"Totie," a nickname from her childhood days based on her
mispronunciation of Sophie.

Being in clubs all the time gave her few romantic options:
patrons, club owners, or other comedians. She opted for door
#3 and married fellow laugh getter George William Johnston
Jr. in 1950. Over time, "Georgie" became her musical director
and the father of their two daughters. That means we can all
blame George for causing the youthfully thin Sophie to gain
pregnancy weight and never get it off. So in turn we should
blame Totie for being smart enough to put it in the act and
make it work. She was the original plump girl who wasn't
ashamed.

Fields bursts onto the national scene after Ed Sullivan
discovered her in the Copacabana and featured her on his top-
rated, star-making CBS variety show almost twenty times.
She went on to appear on *The Mike Douglas Show, The Merv
Griffin Show, The Glen Campbell Show, The Tonight Show
with Johnny Carson, Here's Lucy,* and a variety of programs of
the day. She played the Catskills in the early '60s when women
were more or less eye candy and not vessels of opinions.
Fields had things to say. She also had musings better suited
for the written page. In 1972, she plucked an author feather
and put it in her cap when she wrote a diet book, entitled *I
Think I'll Start on Monday: The Official 8 ½ Oz. Mashed
Potato Diet.*

Fields was a diabetic and suffered multiple heath issues,
including a leg amputation in 1976, two heart attacks in
1977, and a breast removal that same year. Yet she continued
to perform and incorporate these bad breaks into her act,
often bringing crowds to tears . . . then laughter. During her

HBO special for *Standing Room Only,* she stood up from her wheelchair and proclaimed, "I've waited all my life to say this . . . I weigh less than Elizabeth Taylor."

In 1978, the American Guild of Variety Artists voted Totie Fields "Entertainer of the Year" and "Female Comedy Star of the Year." As she was preparing to show what all the fuss was about with a two-week engagement at the Sahara Hotel in Las Vegas, Fields suffered a fatal pulmonary embolism and was whisked to Sunrise Hospital and Medical Center where she soon died. It was August 2, 1978, the day before she was to start her run.

Some have attributed Fields's other complications to plastic surgeries. Whatever the case, Totie Fields opened the comedic door for the sexually active and conscious plus-size female. She told self-deprecating jokes about her weight while at the same time flirting with the listener. However, when it came to real life, Totie loved her some Georgie. Her true wish was fulfilled when she was buried alongside him at Mount Sinai Cemetery upon his death in 1995. She had been laid to rest in Las Vegas. Now that's romance.

ELAINE MAY

Sophistication had its place too, as was evident in the teaming of Mike Nichols and Elaine May. She was from Philly, had trained as an actress, and was a member of the precursor to Second City, the Compass Players, where she met Mike Nichols in the mid-'50s. They formed a partnership and soon became the toast of New York, performing in clubs and making frequent television appearances.

Their brand of cabaret cocktail comedy-infused intelligence, wit, and improvisation was the hallmark of the duo. It was Nichols and May who popularized improvising as a comedy form.

After receiving a Grammy for their album *An Evening with Mike Nichols and Elaine May* in 1962, May moved on to write films, star in them, and direct. She received an Oscar nomination for *Heaven Can Wait* starring Warren Beatty, co-starred in the romantic comedy *The New Leaf* opposite Walter Matthau, and just to show she could fail like any man, she directed the box office catastrophe *Ishtar*.

After that disaster, no studio mounted another Elaine May film.

ANNE MEARA

wo beneficiaries of Nichols and May mainstreaming improvisation were the team of Stiller and Meara. The Irish-Catholic Anne Meara met Jewish Jerry Stiller in the group the Compass Players, which would later be known as Second City. They soon became a team, got married in 1954, and she converted to Judaism. Meara was so devoted to the faith, her passion prompted Stiller to say, "Being married to Anne has made me more Jewish."

The 1960s was the team's golden age. Stiller and Meara were regulars on *The Ed Sullivan Show* and frequently made appearances on other talk and variety shows. As the '70s inched along, the variety-show format showed so many signs of wear it finally tore, and acts like Stiller and Meara stopped getting the steady phone calls. They wrote and performed radio commercials for Blue Nun wine, and in the waning days of variety, the duo had a five-minute syndicated spot that aired right after *Saturday Night Live* on an affiliate in Washington, DC.

Regardless, they were two talented people and continued to work. Jerry Stiller played Frank Costanza on *Seinfeld* and Arthur Spooner on *The King of Queens*. Anne was such a gifted actress she found work in television as well as film, working with acting legends such as Sir Laurence Olivier (*The Boys from Brazil*). She had a recurring role as one of Rhoda's best friends on the CBS sitcom *Rhoda*. As Meara of the famed team became more recognized as Anne Meara, her phone traffic increased. She co-starred as a cook on the hit spin-off *Archie Bunker's Place*. Anne even traded lines with a dubious-looking alien as a grandmother on *Alf.*

An ill-conceived sitcom had the team reuniting for *The Stiller and Meara Show*. In it Stiller played the deputy mayor of New York City married to a TV commercial actress. The viewers of America found it pretty farfetched and kept their dials tuned to something else. The Meara train kept chugging along with recurring parts in *Sex and the City* and her husband's show, *The King of Queens*. In 2007, Anne was consulting director of the Jewish American Princesses, staging live stand-up routines mixed with stories of comedy legends. The year 2010 saw the couple reunited once more for *Stiller & Meara*, their web series for Red Hour Digital, the company owned by their actor-director son, Ben Stiller. Separately or with her partner, comedienne Anne Meara kept audiences laughing and entertained.

CHAPTER 7
Caroling, Caroling

"Comedy is tragedy plus time." **—Carol Burnett**

Most comediennes had what we'll call unique childhoods. Poverty, dysfunctional families, lack of stable living arrangements, and a shady male figure or two make up the kit. Then there's the person. Such circumstances morph individuals and drive them into alternative realities to escape the onslaught of it all. The young create imaginary friends. The older create dead brain cells and pickled livers.

CAROL BURNETT

Alcoholism has taken away from us many great performers. Few found greater talent at the bottom of a bottle. The Burnetts' lust for booze gave us one. Both care providers were drunks, and so little Carol was left with her grandmother to raise her. Turned out granny had plenty of love, but little money, and they ended up in the seedy section of Hollywood, California, in a boarding house with Carol's younger half-sister, Chrissy. In the fourth grade, Carol invented a twin sister named Karen, but not an imaginary twin. This one everybody could see. As Carol recalled, she "fooled the other boarders in the rooming house where we lived by frantically switching clothes and dashing in and out of the house by the fire escape and the front door. Then I became exhausted and Karen mysteriously vanished." That was a lot to go through to suspend belief. Who knows how many were fooled by the panting child's exuberant claim, but Carol thought they bought it and that's all someone looking for attention needs.

Carol Burnett realized she was a comedienne in college. While attending UCLA to study journalism (her mother had told her anybody could write no matter what they looked like), she took a mandatory acting class. In her very first scene in front of the class, Carol got her first big laugh. A junkie was born. She appeared in school productions and got rave notices for her comedic abilities, much to the chagrin of her never-approving mother, who used to whack Carol for making funny faces.

In 1954, Cinderella's fairy godfather showed up. After performing along with some other students at a professor's black-tie party, Carol made her way over to the food table and began stealing cookies to take back to her grandmother. She was caught with her hands in the cookie plate by a man and his wife. Waiting to get balled out and kicked out, Carol was surprised to discover they were fans, and the man wanted to know what she had in store for her future. At the time Carol had only a dream of going to New York to break into musical comedies. The man decided to make that dream come true and offered her and her boyfriend $1,000 a piece to go give it their all. The loan was interest-free, to be repaid in five years and no mention of the man's name was ever to be made. The only other condition was to help somebody else when she could. Carol accepted, and she and boyfriend Don Saroyan (who she married in 1955 and divorced in 1962) dropped out of college and headed for New York.

Carol's first year in the city that never sleeps would've given most fledgling performers nightmares. One thing—her father died of complications from alcohol. She had to deal with that while working the entire year without a gig in show business. Her gig was as a hat-check girl, and they weren't discovering too many of them for stage stardom. The one bright spot of 1955 for Burnett is when somebody came up with the idea to hold a showcase. She lived in a boarding house and the girls there had similar circumstances. So Carol and company invited agents and industry types to The Rehearsal Hall Revue and displayed their talents. Carol got a gig playing the girlfriend to Paul Winchell's dummy, Jerry Mahoney. From there she earned a sitcom spot on the Buddy Hackett one-season laugher, *Stanley*.

Despite breaking in as the love interest to a piece of wood, Carol was on the radar. She gained a reputation as a rising talent on the New York night club scene. By 1957, Carol was performing on *The Tonight Show* and *The Ed Sullivan Show* and was a regular on the game show *Pantomime Quiz*. It was a red-letter year. It was also the year her mother died.

In 1959, Carol Burnett appeared in the smash Broadway musical *Once Upon a Mattress* and became a regular on *The Garry Moore Show*. The year 1962 gave Carol the memory of her first Emmy win, for Outstanding Performance in a Variety or Musical Program or Series. From there it was off to Carnegie Hall to headline along with friend Julie Andrews in *Julie and Carol at Carnegie Hall*. The show won an Emmy. In '63 she hooked up with producer Joe Hamilton and entered into her second marriage. Carol also met Lucille Ball and they became friends until Ball's death in 1989. The relationship was so chummy that Lucy offered to produce a sitcom for Carol under the Desilu banner. Carol thanked her, but opted to do a variety show instead. A tragic side note to their friendship came in the form of a yearly ritual. Ball would routinely send Carol flowers on her birthday. On her fifty-sixth birthday, Carol got the news that Lucy had died, and as she grieved the flowers arrived with a note that read, "Happy Birthday, Kid. Love, Lucy."

The plan to do a variety show was not met with enthusiastic applause from the suits over at CBS. They'd given Carol a one-year contract to do whatever type of show she wanted; little did they suspect she'd choose the variety format. That was the bastion of male performers. Women were guests on such shows, not hosts. It was going to be a big mistake. Carol didn't agree and held them to their written agreement. Her big mistake lasted eleven seasons and received twenty-three Emmys with the cast of Lyle Waggoner, Harvey Korman, Tim Conway, and Vicki Lawrence (who got the job because she looked like a young Carol Burnett).

The Carol Burnett mistake featured parodies of movies, TV shows, and commercials. One sketch was so popular it was spun off into the hit sitcom *Mama's Family* starring Lawrence. Carol's ritual of tugging her ear at the end of each taping to let her grandmother know she was doing fine and happy took on a bittersweet quality when her grandmother died during the show's run. The success stopped in 1978, and Carol moved on to other aspects of her career. She starred in several films playing dramatic roles, guest starred on sitcoms, and returned to the stage to co-star with Rock Hudson in 1985. She even tried to revive the variety show format, but the '60s and '70s were over and so was that genre.

Professionally Carol Burnett lived out her dreams. A longtime fan of the ABC soap opera *All My Children,* Carol had a part written for her by show creator Agnes Nixon. Privately her life was not so dreamy. Her marriage to Joe Hamilton ended in divorce in 1984, and Hamilton died of cancer in 1991. The union produced three children. Daughter Carrie had become addicted to drugs and died at age thirty-eight of lung and brain cancer. The two had written a play together that made it to Broadway and starred Linda Lavin and Michele Pawk (who won a Tony Award for her performance). Carol sued the *National Enquirer* for reporting she was drunk in public with Henry Kissinger and won. That was a major decision and put tabloids on alert that some celebrities do more than tug their ears. They bite—a bite to the tune of $800,000. Carol Burnett knew a funny joke when she cashed in on it.

VIKKI LAWRENCE

orn in Inglewood, California, comedienne/actress/singer Vicki Ann Axelrad got her big show business break when she sent Carol Burnett and her producers a letter. She attached a picture of herself, which clearly showed how much she looked like Burnett. That photo landed her a job on *The Carol Burnett Show* and she did the entire eleven seasons and got her own spin-off (*Mama's Family*).

Lawrence was married twice. First husband, songwriter Bobby Russell, wrote her the song "The Night the Lights Went Out in Georgia" (it was first offered to Cher, but Sonny turned it down), which became a number-one hit in 1973. The two were divorced in early '74, and she married make-up artist Al Schultz in late '74. She and Al had two kids and a life in Hawaii after *The Carol Burnett Show* left the air. They returned to the States when NBC offered her *Mama's Family* and she's found herself in syndication heaven.

CHARO

haro wasn't a comedienne by any stretch of the imagination, but during the '60s she was definitely comic relief. The Latin entertainer and "cuchi-cuchi" girl would pop up on virtually every show on the air, say "cuchi-cuchi" while gyrating and going up and down, grin broadly, and then babble intentionally unintelligible Spanglish. In other words, the sexy Latina bride of Xavier Cugat was good for a hearty stereotypical laugh.

CHAPTER 8

Breathe in, Laugh Out

"Reality is a crutch for people who can't handle drugs." —**Lily Tomlin**

Rowan & Martin's Laugh-In took everybody by surprise. It was a combination of Your Show of Shows and what most non-drug users in 1967 thought an acid trip must be like. Ratings shot through the roof for a show that skewered everything American: the Vietnam War, the civil rights movement, the government, the drug culture, etc. Its title came from a takeoff of the then popular term for disobedience—"sit-in." Former presidents, future presidents, sports heroes, movie stars, and even Carol Channing made an appearance on the NBC weekly "Sock It to Me" hour. Comediennes were prevalent in all six seasons: Eileen Brennan, Mitzi McCall, Chelsea Brown, Teresa Graves, Pamela Rodgers, Ann Elder, Nancie Phillips, Barbara Sharma, Moosie Drier, Patti Deutsch, Lisa Farringer, Sarah Kennedy, and Donna Jean Young. Its principle four comediennes became famous.

JUDY CARNE

The "Sock It to Me" girl was born Joyce Audrey Botterill in London. Her dad was a fruit merchant, and Laugh-In was just what she needed after years of playing second bananas on forgettable sitcoms like *Fair Exchange* (a teenage exchange student), *The Baileys of Balboa* (a commodore's daughter on a show that wasn't about the commodore), *Love on a Rooftop* (the romantic interest to Peter Duel), and in real life, as Mrs. Burt Reynolds from 1963 to 1965. In 1967, her status was elevated and she became an NBC television star. Every time Carne was tricked into saying "Sock it to me!" she was doused in water or had something else dumped on her. She was the poster child for abusive comedy for the first two seasons, refused to renew her contract at the end of the second season, yet appeared in and left at the end of the third season, earning her the wrath of producer George Schlatter.

Carne went on to be a fixture on daytime game shows and a busload of guest-starring roles. She later wrote a book describing her drug problems and conflicts about her bisexuality. She also detailed her failed marriage to Burt Reynolds.

LILY TOMLIN

Mary Jean "Lily" Tomlin joined *Laugh-In* in the middle of the third season. The show was by then firmly established as a hit, and the Detroit-born stand-up comedienne gained national exposure on the show as the persnickety telephone switchboard operator Ernestine; Edith Ann, the know-it-all five-year-old in the oversize chair; and a variety of other characters Tomlin unleashed. She was arguably the program's first breakout star, with her characters living strong lives outside of *Laugh-In*. AT&T offered her a half million bucks to have Ernestine in a phone company commercial. Tomlin turned it down, citing the artistic integrity of her creation as the reason not to become a corporate shill. Edith Ann was later used in three animated specials, and Tomlin's groundbreaking characters of Rick and Tommy Velour represented the first time a female performer broke out in drag and they were summoned again and again.

However, Tomlin was more than a sketch show phenom.

After her run on *Laugh-In,* Lily Tomlin went on a medium attack: recordings, stage, writing, film, and more television. Her comedy albums are two of the top three by a female comedian. Tomlin made record-breaking televised prime-time specials and after-school specials; she did one-woman shows on Broadway and films that people stood in line to see. In 1977, *Time* magazine dubbed Lily "America's New Queen of Comedy." She did animation voice-overs, had recurring parts on *Will & Grace, Murphy Brown,* and *Desperate Housewives,* as well as being a regular on *The West Wing.* Her exemplary career and massive range has garnered Lily Tomlin four Emmys, two Tonys, a Grammy, two Peabodys, and a Mark Twain Award, as well as an Oscar nomination.

Tomlin has always been upfront about her sexuality. She's appeared in a number of gay and lesbian productions and has been longtime partners creatively and personally with writer-producer Jan Wagner, whom she met in 1971 after seeing her work on an after-school special. Though her orientation was known throughout the entertainment industry, Tomlin came out officially in 2001. She's battled those who would poke fun at her lifestyle, such as *Tonight Show* host Johnny Carson, and did some joke poking herself at straight actors who make a big deal about playing gay. Tomlin turned that mindset on its ear when she once parodied a gay actor with a straight role dilemma. "How did it feel to play a heterosexual? I've seen these women all my life, I know how they walk, I know how they talk."

GOLDIE HAWN

First-season cast member Goldie Hawn never looked like she was hiding anything, especially when her doofus dancer persona sported her signature bikini and body paint on *Laugh-In.* She was known as the era's dumb blonde, breaking into uncontrollable giggling during a set-up joke, then nailing a polished performance immediately after. Raised Jewish, Hawn balanced that faith with the teachings of Buddhism and a heavy dose of being a free spirit. This quality wasn't lost on Hollywood producers when they summoned her for a string of cinematic hits. Of her films, 1969's *Cactus Flower* won her an Academy Award for Best Supporting Actress.

Hawn did comedies (*There's a Girl in My Soup* and *Butterflies Are Free*) and flexed her dramatic muscles (*Shampoo* and *The Sugarland Express*). Following a break in the action to reproduce with second husband, Bill Hudson, Goldie made a resurgence with Chevy Chase in *Foul Play.* A nice run was followed up by a couple of flops, and Hawn decided to make her way into producing. The result of that maneuver was another string of hits (*Private Benjamin, Seems Like Old Times*, and *Protocol*).

Hawn's popularity never suffered even through her various breaks and unconventional moves. In 1972, the hippie recorded a well-received country album. In 1983, she began publically shacking up with actor Kurt Russell and raising a family (son Oliver Hudson has stated he considers Russell to be his father) minus the ceremony or rings. In 1985, the free spirit posed for *Playboy's* cover at age thirty-nine. She's been attacked for her pro-Israeli stance by Palestinian groups. She's been blasted for her Hawn Foundation, which teaches fourth through seventh graders the Buddhist technique of mindfulness training (in other words, being aware of the present moment in everyday life).

Through it all, it's Goldie Hawn's talent that has given her one of the most enduring careers of any multimedia comedienne. Her films made money (*Bird on a Wire* and *House Sitter*). Her productions made money (*Something to Talk About,* starring sometimes film comedienne Julia Roberts). Even her reproductions made money (her sons, Wyatt Russell and Oliver Hudson, are accomplished actors, and her daughter is title-topping actress Kate Hudson).

JO ANNE WORLEY

Jo Anne Worley said she was so loud as a kid, she'd lip-synch the hymns in church so she wouldn't drown everybody out. She put that volume to good use on *Laugh-In,* after being discovered over the course of about forty appearances on *The Merv Griffin Show.* Merv's people discovered her doing her nightclub act in Greenwich Village. She'd gotten there via Broadway, the Pasadena Playhouse, and the Pickwick Players. So when she got on *Laugh-In,* she was a seasoned vet ready for her close-up.

Worley's close-up lasted three seasons. She was best remembered for saying "Bo-ring" at the top of her lungs and using her loud operatic voice. When she left the show, Worley's busy career consisted of guest-starring roles, voice-overs, game shows, cartoons, movies, video games, and theater.

RUTH BUZZI

Ruth Buzzi holds the distinction of appearing in every episode of *Laugh-In,* including the pilot and a later televised special. Raised in a rock house overlooking the ocean, Buzzi's father was famous stone carver Angelo Peter Buzzi, whose works adorn New York's Penn Station and Natural History Museum. Fittingly enough, Ruth graduated from Stonington High School, where she was a cheerleader, and at age seventeen went to the Pasadena Playhouse. There she studied dance, acting, voice, and cosmetology (the latter in case the first three didn't pan out). By age nineteen, she began her first of what turned into nineteen roles in musical comedy productions, beginning with crooner Rudy Vallee.

Ruth teamed up with Dom Deluise as assistant to his magician, and the mock gained them national exposure on *The Garry Moore Show* and *Entertainers with Carol Burnett.* Bob Fosse plucked her up to be featured in his Broadway production of *Sweet Charity.* Soon after this break, she got her big shot as a cast member on *Laugh-In.* The show showcased her vast variety of characters, but it was her old woman that kept popping up in places beyond the NBC hit. Gladys Ormphby, who wore a hair net and had a itchy purse arm, pelted most of the honorees on *The Dean Martin Celebrity Roasts* as well as Martin himself. Buzzi herself was far from old when she made this character a weekly favorite, and after the show's run she stayed active in films, commercials, voice-overs, music videos, frequent appearances on *Sesame Street,* and her roots of musical comedy revues.

Like many of the comediennes from *Laugh-In,* Buzzi's mantle is packed. She's won a Golden Globe, a Clio Award, been a five-time nominee for an Emmy, has a Lifetime Achievement Award, been inducted into the Television Hall of Fame, and is the only white woman to win an NAACP Image Award.

CHAPTER 9
Whatchu Talkin' About

"I'm nervous as a whore in church." **—LaWanda Page**

The civil rights movement was over. The sexual revolution was over. California didn't break off and fall into the sea. It was the 1970s and time for television to grow up. Women were now walking and talking like real women and not a male fantasy *Stepford Wives* ala *That Girl* and *Gidget.* These new independent models were spewing real ideas and questioning the knowledge of their menfolk.

Bea Arthur's *Maude* had a deep voice and the stature to intimidate anybody who didn't like what it was enunciating. The sitcom dealt squarely with abortion, racism, sexism, infidelity, and homosexuality; in other words, just another typical night in front of the set in the '70s.

Typical if it was a Norman Lear offering. Stormin' Norman never saw a taboo he didn't like and along with his partner, Bud Yorkin, had the majority of television's other producers thinking likewise. On *The Jeffersons,* wife Isabel Sanford talked back to her successful and upwardly mobile husband. On that same show Marla Gibbs the maid also talked back to Sanford's successful and upwardly mobile husband. While on *What's Happening,* Shirley Hemphill, the waitress, talked back to everybody.

SHIRLEY HEMPHILL

Hemphill wanted her talking to mean something, and her destiny was clear when she sent a comedy cassette tape of herself to Flip Wilson. The comedy routines she'd recorded on a borrowed tape recorder got her noticed by the top-rated variety-show host. Wilson liked it so much that he flew her out to California to a taping of his self-titled show. He got her a dozen roses and her own recorder for future cassette tapings. After that experience, Shirley (as she was often billed) was determined to be a comedy star. So she got a job as a waitress at a fast-food joint during the day and worked her comedy craft at night.

Shirley gained attention from other media types too. Soon she was adding guest-starring roles to her resume on shows like *Good Times.* Then came the part she became identified with—"Shirley" on Eric Monte's *What's Happening!!,* which ran from '76 to '79.

"When you watched What's Happening!! *you couldn't wait for her to get on the screen. When she walked up to the table you were already laughing. It's one thing to say the line. It's another thing to nail it. Shirley would nail it."* —Myra J.

Following its cancelation, Hemphill got her own sitcom, *One in a Million,* in 1980. On it she played the boss, the result of going from being a taxi driver to inheriting a huge corporation. The show lasted thirteen episodes. So it was back to nightclubs and guest-starring spots in shows like *Trapper John, MD,* and *The Love Boat.*

Then lightning struck twice. In 1985, Shirley reprised her role on *What's Happening Now.* It featured an unknown Martin Lawrence (who she'd loan money to during his lean times) and ran until 1988. When the show was canceled a second time, she did some guest-starring roles (*The Wayans Bros., The Sinbad Show,* and *Martin*) but mainly returned to the stand-up stage, headlining regularly at the world-famous

Comedy Store in Hollywood. She also highlighted her hilarious stand-up chops on *The Tonight Show, Evening at the Improv,* and assorted BET comedy entries.

Jus June recalls one: "Shirley says to me about a young stripper in the dressing room, when we taped BET's pay-per-view comic/stripper thing. 'June, where would you go in your mind at twenty-one to decide you wanna show your titties? I've never been there.'"

In 1994, Shirley made her first movie, Chris Rock's *CB4*. Her second film, entitled *Shoot the Moon*, came two years later.

Unfortunately illness intervened, sidelining her from working. Shirley had gotten so depressed from this turn of events that she changed her phone number and refused to give her friends her new one. She wasn't fond of pity parties. Her health declined, which wasn't helped by her avoidance of surgery to relieve any pain. She wasn't fond of being cut into either. She became so isolated that it wasn't until days later on December 10, 1999, that Shirley's gardener peeked into her window expecting to see the former live wire tooling around in her walker or staring outside with her sunken jaws, but instead discovered her laying prone on the floor. Shirley Hemphill had died of a heart attack caused by kidney failure and obesity. She was fifty-two years old.

"She so funny, I loved that woman, good spirit too. She didn't have the big head and made any audience laugh, black, white, Mexican, Jews, gentiles, infidels, Muslims, midgets . . . some of these folks have big heads and little jokes." —Jus June

The loveable waitress on *What's Happening!!* wasn't the only one mouthing off. Raunchy, nightclub comedienne LaWanda Page's Aunt Esther was stealing scenes even from the great Redd Foxx. He couldn't have been happier. When Page first read for the part, the show's producers started thumbing through their Rolodex for a quick replacement. However, Foxx insisted his handpicked leading lady was staying, coached her himself, and the rest is junkyard history.

LAWANDA PAGE

lberta Peal was born on October 19, 1920, in Cleveland, Ohio, and was raised in St. Louis, Missouri, where she first met Redd Foxx (at the time named John Sanford) as a preteen and grew up with him. They went to the same school and were very close friends. It was coincidental that they each got into comedy (on separate occasions), but not coincidental that Foxx looked out for his former chum when the time came.

Initially LaWanda performed as "The Bronze Goddess of Fire," where her act consisted of fire-eating by the "goddess." For an eye-opener, she'd strike matches with the tips of her fingers. In the late '60s and early '70s, she became an active recording artist for Laff Records, putting out product with subtle titles like the bestselling gold record *Watch It, Sucka.* She was raw, uncut, and uncensored.

To the urban audience, the raunchy LaWanda was "The Queen of Comedy." To the mainstream crowd, Aunt Esther was "The Black Queen of Comedy." To comediennes, she was the yardstick.

On *Sanford and Son,* Aunt Esther was Fred Sanford's sister-in-law. His wife was dead, but Esther made him feel like he had to live up to her obviously lofty principles. Bible-toting and sanctimonious in nature, Aunt Esther was in church even when she wasn't. You could practically see her cooling herself with a fan from the pews whenever things got hot, as they always did when she entered Fred Sanford's junkyard lot and house of business. She'd call him a "fish-eyed fool" and a "heathen" and we'd roar.

"Her comedy was genderless. You forgot a woman was saying all this." —Ajai Sanders

Everybody knew an Aunt Esther in real life and LaWanda Page embodied them all, creating one of the most distinctive sitcom characters of all time.

The irony of Aunt Esther was that nobody wanted her

except Redd Foxx. Page herself was frustrated with the LA club circuit and was about to drop out of show biz and move back to St. Louis to tend to her ailing mother, until Foxx offered her the role of a lifetime. The suits loved the character, but not Page. She'd never done TV before and was unfamiliar with its staging and rhythm. Despite agreeing to the casting initially, they wanted to backtrack and get a trained thespian. Trained thespians weren't up Redd Foxx's alley. He wanted funny. So he rebuked their rebuking and worked with Page until the Aunt Esther in her personality appeared when a camera was trained on her and the red light came on.

We all owe Foxx a thank-you. Because of his stubbornness and diligence, LaWanda Page not only became indelible on *Sanford and Son* and its spin-offs *Sanford* and *Sanford Arms,* she went on to bring big laughs to other shows: *Diff'rent Strokes, Amen, 227, Family Matters*, with frequent appearances on *The Dean Martin Celebrity Roasts* and *Martin*.

"We had a brief friendship I will always remember," Miss Laura Hayes said, "and it began with being on *Martin* together. She was giving me game as we was on the set about television and the whole thing and being a female and about your managers, how they running your shit. They'll treat you like a little bitch too, y'know. But the whole time she's giving me game. Then she invited me to her home and you know she lived down in the hood.

"The couple of times I went to visit with her, that's when I found out she did stand-up comedy. She was telling me about the men who supported her, Redd Foxx and all them. You know, she was facing the same old isms back then. Woo, and she was hot too. I saw this picture of her, I think she, I don't want to say, did some stripping. But they didn't call it that."

LaWanda Page recorded bits for musical artists (RuPaul), made commercials for the masses (Church's Chicken), and appeared in movies where she stole her scenes (*Friday, My Blue Heaven, Shakes the Clown*, and *Don't Be a Menace to South Central While Drinking Your Juice in the Hood*).

LaWanda Page had a stroke in 1996 that all but wiped her out. In '97 she had an angioplasty to widen the arteries in her legs.

"The nicest woman; gave me great advice. One of the things she said to me, 'You're a stand-up. You're good and a lot of opportunities are going to come your way. You'll get offers to do TV. You'll get offers to do film, but never give up your stand-up because as long as you can tell jokes, you can always work. Sometimes doing TV is too much mustard for the hot dog.' I never forgot that and I saw her years later when she was in a wheelchair. I went up to her and I thanked her."

—Myra J.

On September 14, 2002, LaWanda was admitted to Centinela Hospital, where she had a heart attack and died of complications from diabetes. The queen abdicated the throne at eighty-one years of age.

LIZ TORRES

L iz Torres was Puerto Rican. She was all her life. She was even Puerto Rican when the comedienne gained recognition on the Cloris Leachman sitcom *Phyllis,* playing the very un-Puerto Rican Julie Erskine. A product of the Bronx and a post-WWII baby (she was born in 1947), Liz was a first-generation Puerto Rican American after her parents immigrated. She got into show business by working the New York club circuit with her buddy Bette Midler. All the late nights out in the streets paid off when Liz was seen doing her stand-up routine by a booker for *The Tonight Show* in 1971. Following her appearance, she guest starred on sitcoms like *All in the Family* and, in '73, played Morticia in the musical *Addams Family Fun House.* Then it was *Phyllis* in '75–'76 and a co-starring stint opposite Marla Gibbs on the unsuccessful *Jeffersons* spin-off *Checkin' In,* in 1981.

Liz Torres's resume boasts over one hundred guest-starring appearances and several recurring roles. She received an Emmy Award nomination for the sitcom *The Famous Teddy Z* and got a Bravo Award for that same show. Other honors came and went, but it wasn't until her part on *The John Larroquette Show* that Torres could finally look a Nielsen box right dead in the eye. She landed on a hit series as a regular and garnered an Emmy, Golden Globe, and American Comedy Award nominations for her outstanding performances. She was a semi-regular on *Gilmore Girls,* a recurring character on *Ugly Betty,* and a guest star on *Desperate Housewives.* Liz also made over fifty films since her cinematic debut in 1969 in the low-budget flick *Utterly Without Redeeming Social Value.* She made her Broadway debut in 1994 and performed for the King Hassan II of Morocco. During the first National Hispanic Week celebration, Liz received and accepted an invitation from the Jimmy Carter White House.

The 1970s was the decade when minorities were reaping the benefits of the civil rights movement. America wanted the world to see how much progress had been made and minorities were highly visible in the mediums, especially film and television. There weren't enough comediennes, as far as the industry was concerned, and so the demand for minority talent expanded the parameters of who did comedy. The majority of the comedic actresses working in '70s sitcoms were in fact serious actresses with a gift for comedy.

ISABEL SANFORD

"She wore a necklace that said, "Sexy Bitch," all diamonds."
—Robin Montague

Isabel Sanford (*The Jeffersons*) worked in theater in the 1960s. In '68 she appeared as the maid in the Sidney Poitier vehicle Guess *Who's Coming to Dinner.* Norman Lear cast her as Louise Jefferson in *All in the Family,* a part she almost rejected when she got a bucket of KFC sent to her dressing room. Lear claimed the chicken was a way of saying congratulations. He apologized if there was any offense. He said he did it to everybody. In this case he had done it to the first black actress to win an Emmy for Best Lead Actress. The year was 1981. After the show shut down, she was so type-cast as "Weezy" she capitalized on it by doing guest-starring parts and cameos with Sherman Hemsley, until she died of a cardiac arrest at the age of eighty-seven on July 9, 2004.

MARLA GIBBS

Marla Gibbs (*The Jeffersons*) was born Margaret Theresa Bradley on June 14, 1931, and worked as a reservations agent for United Airlines before moving from Detroit to LA and becoming an actress. She gained her formal training in Watts at the Mafundi Institute and the Watts Writers' Workshop, and received strong notices in a number of theater productions before getting the part of Florence Johnston on *The Jeffersons*. The long-running CBS show made her an international celebrity. Once *The Jeffersons* was abruptly canceled in 1985, Marla Gibbs produced and starred in the sitcom *227* for NBC for five seasons. She also continued to work in television and film, dramatic as well as comedic. Gibbs owned a jazz and supper club and from '91 to '99 and released a music CD in 2006.

JACKEE HARRY

Gibbs's rival on her sitcom *227* came from theater and a soap opera before taking up residence as Sandra Clark. Thanks to that journey, Jacqueline Yvonne "Jackee" Harry became the first African American female to win an Emmy for Best Supporting Actress in a Comedy Series. She followed that up with two NAACP Image Awards for her stint as Lisa Landry on *Sister, Sister* and a return to the theater.

ESTHER ROLLE

Esther Rolle (*Good Times*) attended Yale University, was the director of the Asadata Dafora's dance troupe, and appeared in theater productions with titles like *The Blacks, The Crucible,* and *Blues for Mr. Charlie.* Not exactly the happy-go-lucky stuff of a comedienne. That didn't come along until the role of Florida Evans, the maid of *Maude,* and a spin-off of that show. *Good Times* made her a household name, but she vacated those households when she found the character of J. J. Evans (Jimmie Walker) to be a tad bit too degrading for her taste and left the show. Her post–*Good Times* career consisted of guest-starring roles, made-for-TV movies, and even a psychic hotline. Cinematically, Rolle is best remembered as Aunt Sarah in the 1997 film *Rosewood.* She worked until her death from complications caused by diabetes in 1998 at the age of seventy-eight.

JA'NET DUBOIS

You can't think about *Good Times* without thinking about Willona, Florida's neighbor and friend. Ja'net Dubois brought the sassy sidekick to life after getting Norman Lear's attention from a guest-starring spot she did on *Sanford and Son.* Once King Lear gave her a break, the singer-songwriter (she co-wrote the theme to *The Jeffersons*) took off. Not only did she anchor *Good Times* when Esther Rolle departed from the show, Dubois carved out an impressive career guest starring on a number of sitcoms, including *Martin,* where she reprised the Willona character, *Moesha, The Steve Harvey Show,* and *The Wayans Bros.* She appeared in *Charlie's Angels, Full Throttle,* and *I'm Gonna Git You Sucka.* Dubois won an Emmy for *Other People's Children* and two Emmys for her voice-over work on *The PJs.*

MABEL KING

Mabel King (*What's Happening!!*) was born Donnie Mabel Elizabeth Washington and became a nightclub and gospel singer. She began her acting career in 1966 when King played Maria in *Porgy and Bess*. From there she did Broadway (*Hello Dolly!, Don't Play Us Cheap,* and *The Wiz*) and film (reprising her roles in theatrical versions of the latter two plays, as well as the horror flick *Ganja & Hess* playing a queen, *Scott Joplin* playing a madam, and *The Bingo Long Traveling All-Stars & Motor Kings* playing Bertha). In 1976, King got the co-starring role of the mother in *What's Happening!!,* but left in '78 after disputes regarding the future direction of the show. She continued to work in movies (*The Jerk* as Steve Martin's mother) and on Broadway until a stroke in 1989 forced her into the Motion Picture & Television Country House and Hospital. There she battled diabetes, losing an arm and both of her legs, finally succumbing to the disease on November 9, 1999 (one month before *What's Happening!!* co-star Shirley Hemphill's death).

THERESA MERRITT

Theresa Merritt (*That's My Mama*) was a Virginia-born stage actress and singer with an impressive resume of theatrical accomplishments, including a Tony Award nomination for *Ma Rainey's Black Bottom*. She replaced Mabel King in *The Wiz,* but left the production because of the demands it placed on her voice. After playing Clifton Davis's mother, Eloise Curtis, for thirty-nine episodes on ABC, Merritt worked in television and film until her death on June 12, 1998, of skin cancer.

SYLVIA TRAYMORE MORRISON

The entire era was unconventional. Ever hear of Sylvia Traymore Morrison? You should've. Sylvia was the sole black female impressionist of her time. Her repertoire was envious. She could imitate men as well as women. She was placed in high-profile slot after high-profile slot, but the cards were not stacked during her time for Sylvia to be a name poised on our lips in our time. Odd because during that time she was on everybody else's.

"I remember coming offstage the first night at the Comedy Store," Morrison reminisced. "I was number nineteen. There were so many comics there that night. Of course I was the only black woman. Quite frankly I don't remember any females being in line with me that day. When I got offstage, they said the owner, Mitzi, wanted to see me. I went to talk to Mitzi. She said, 'I absolutely love you. These people love you.' She told me to go to the West Hollywood [Comedy] Store. She gave me the information she wanted me to have. I remember everybody that night saying, Mitzi don't call everybody over. You got to be real, real good for her to decide to call you out."

A regular spot at the Comedy Store during this period was a big career boost. People who mattered frequented the club on Sunset Blvd. and being seen by those right people could take you to the next step, that is, if the rest of the people got wind of it. There was a high-profile roast being given for Muhammad Ali and the potential hosts were Dick Gregory, Frankie Crocker, or Richard Pryor. For some reason, none of them could make it, but *Jet* magazine was there. Unfortunately the reporter forgot something that day.

"Well, when they talked about it afterward you think they would've said, 'Well, none of them did it, but they found a woman by the name of Sylvia Traymore who's the only black female. . .' This is *Jet* magazine! For God's sake they didn't even mention me. They wanted to announce all the big stars that were there for Muhammad Ali."

Somebody took notice.

"I did my impression of him [Ali] in front of him and he came out on that stage, grabbed my hand, and took me with him. And I know this is what nailed it—he held my hand up in the air and he said, 'A woman doing me—that's awesome.'"

The Greatest wasn't the only instant fan. NBC was also in

the house and the SNL rep liked what they saw.

"The reason I got the job at *Saturday Night Live* was because of the Muhammad Ali roast. I got a standing ovation there."

Things were moving so fast, like most of show business, it all became a blur. Sylvia's credits grew and she was even a client of the legendary Redd Foxx, but comedy is fickle and sometimes even those most talented are relegated to trivia question status. Sometimes it's timing; other times that talent wasn't designated to be pushed, for whatever reason. Then there is lack of imagination on the part of the image makers. For every household name that sprang from this time frame, there are dozens more whose names never saw the appropriate light of day. A female impressionist of black skin might've been too novel for anyone to fully commit to at the time.

"It's amazing that everything I did in my young career," Morrison said, "I never had a contract. I didn't have a contract with Whitney Houston. I didn't even have a contract with *Saturday Night Live*. I didn't have a contract when I was in a Miss Black America Pageant. The only contract I signed was with Redd Foxx as my manager, and to be honest with you, I don't even know what the contract said. It was Redd Foxx."

BEA ARTHUR

Born Jewish, Bernice Frankel changed her name to Bea Arthur when she married fellow World War II Marine Robert Alan Aurthur (she altered the spelling). Bea was a typist and truck driver during her thirty months in the Corps and got into show biz when she left, cutting her theatrical teeth on Broadway in *The Three Penny Opera, Fiddler on the Roof,* and *Mame* (she won a Tony Award for her performance as Vera Charles). She went on to win Emmys for *Maude* and *The Golden Girls. Maude* was such a groundbreaking, influential show that it's been said it swayed the United States Supreme Court in their ruling in regard to *Roe vs. Wade* after seeing the *Maude* episodes on abortion where Maude herself decides to get one because of her advanced age. Arthur stayed active, performing on TV, film, and stage until her death from cancer on April 25, 2009.

JEAN STAPLETON

Jean Stapleton (*All in the Family*) was brought into the world as Jeanne Murray on January 19, 1923. Like most of her comedic peers on television, she was a product of Broadway musicals. The part of Edith Bunker on *All in the Family* got her three Emmys and two Golden Globe Awards. Her long-running career consisted of movies and television where Stapleton was able to show off her dramatic and comedy chops. She retired in 2001.

CLORIS LEACHMAN

Cloris Leachman has a career loaded with awards: one Oscar, one daytime Emmy, and a whopping eight prime-time Emmys (more than any other performer). She studied at the Actors Studio under Elia Kazan and did early TV such as *Suspense Theater, The Twilight Zone,* and *Alfred Hitchcock Presents*. She made movies with directors as diverse as Mel Brooks and Robert Aldrich. Leachman competed on *Dancing with the Stars* as the show's oldest contestant, and she is a confirmed agnostic. When her son, Bryan, died of an apparent drug overdose (cocaine) Leachman said, "I've been so relieved and so grateful not to have a God to believe in."

VALERIE HARPER

Valerie Harper gained fame for playing Jewish girlfriend Rhoda Morgenstern. The actress is actually French-British and got her start in show business as a chorus girl on Broadway in the late 1950s. After years on the Great White Way and in low-budget films, Harper was approached to play Rhoda, first on *The Mary Tyler Moore Show* from

1970 to 1974, then on the spin-off *Rhoda* from 1974 to 1978. Veteran comedienne Nancy Walker benefited greatly from this arrangement. She was cast as Ida Morgenstern , Rhoda's mother, and appeared on both *The Mary Tyler Moore Show* and *Rhoda*. After collecting four Emmys and a Golden Globe for the character, Valerie Harper landed her own series, *Valerie,* on NBC. Unfortunately there was a salary dispute and Harper sued the network and producers, eventually winning against the producers, but being replaced on the show by fellow Broadway actress Sandy Duncan.

MARY TYLER MOORE

M ary Tyler Moore can be credited with much of this success. The former Capri girl from *The Dick Van Dyke Show* was the hub and had a cast that walked away with so many Emmys you'd thought they'd phoned in the orders: Cloris Leachman, Valerie Harper, Georgina Engels, Betty White, and of course Mare.

She also broke another mold and separated herself from her comedic peers in that Mary Tyler Moore's real name is Mary Tyler Moore. The eldest sibling and offspring of English-Irish parents, she was reared Catholic in Brooklyn, New York, and then migrated West, where she was educated in Los Angeles and Los Feliz, California. Mary's professional career began at seventeen as the dancing elf Happy Hotpoint for appliance commercials in the '50s, and was famously rejected to play Danny Thomas's daughter because her nose was too small. She bounced back from that one by getting a part in a detective series where all you saw were her legs and all you heard was her voice. She was the receptionist. Moore did sitcoms (*The Tab Hunter Show*), westerns (*Overland Trail* and *Wanted: Dead or Alive*), and stuff near the beach (*Surfside Six, 77 Sunset Strip,* and *Hawaiian Eye*).

In 1961, Carl Reiner approached her about doing a show modeled after his own writing experiences, but it would star Dick Van Dyke. They'd even name the show after the former radio disc jockey, and CBS wanted Moore to play his wife. Despite the fact that the thirty-five-year-old Van Dyke thought twenty-four-year-old Moore (who was lying—she was twenty-three) was too young for the part, she got the role of Laura Petrie, Rob's housekeeping, child-rearing spouse. The show ran for the five years Reiner promised. During that time, she helped the sale of Capri pants to go up by her frequent wearing of them on the show, and she became an international star because of it. Moore also won an Emmy and fought diabetes.

Like most TV stars, Moore wanted movies. The compliment wasn't returned. She made her debut in a flick titled *X-15* (good luck finding that one) in 1961. From there she was signed to a contract with Universal to work in a bunch of movies leading up to Julie Andrews's *Thoroughly Modern Millie* (1967) and her co-starring break with Elvis Presley in *Change of Habit* in 1969. The break broke her film career. It was a financial and critical flop. She wouldn't make another feature-length film for over a decade. Turns out she wouldn't have to for a while.

In 1969, Moore founded MTM Enterprises. In 1970, Mary and husband number two, Grant Tinker, pitched CBS a show about a single career girl working in a newsroom. *The Mary Tyler Moore Show* was in the top 20 for six seasons. In season seven, it slipped to #39 and was canceled at the request of the producers, who didn't want the legacy of the show tainted by becoming insignificant and wished away. They were probably also considering the legacy of MTM, which produced *Hill Street Blues, WKRP in Cincinnati* (starring sexy, Loni Anderson), *The Bob Newhart Show, Newhart, Phyllis, Rhoda,* and the mother ship—Mary's show. That show won three Emmys for Outstanding Comedy Series over the course of its run, and the cast won multiples every season; the show sprung series for all of its principle players: Ed Asner (*Lou Grant*), Cloris Leachman (*Phyllis*), Valerie Harper (*Rhoda*), Gavin MacLeod (*The Love Boat*), Betty White (*The Betty White Show*), Ted Knight (*Too Close for Comfort*), and John

Amos (*Good Times*). The only one who didn't fare well after *The Mary Tyler Moore Show* was Mary Tyler Moore.

Moore's career, as well as her life, was a series of ups and downs. On TV she couldn't reinvent the magic after '77. She did a sitcom named *Mary* that lasted for three episodes. They retooled it and turned it into *The Mary Tyler Moore Hour.* That lasted for three months. Then she made a musical special for CBS that even Moore says will probably never be seen again. She did theater (*Whose Life Is It Anyway*) in 1980, and during that decade her production company produced five plays, but her marriage was rocky and she and Tinker divorced the following year. Moore was nominated for an Academy Award for her work in the Robert Redford film *Ordinary People* in 1980, but that was also the year her only son, Richie (from husband number one, Richard Carlton Meeker) shot himself in the head with a shotgun at age twenty-four. It was ruled an accident and the brand was discontinued due to its "hairpin trigger," but that didn't ease the pain of the already alcoholic Mary. The late '80s saw her back on Broadway for another minor success, but 2003 was not such a fortunate outing. While doing preview shows for Neil Simon's *Rose's Dilemma,* Moore received a note from the hit playwright, saying, "Either learn your lines or get out of my play." She quit. The time was filled with guest-starring roles on sitcoms and reunion specials with either Dick Van Dyke or Valerie Harper.

Moore's time away from the spotlight has been a benefit for sufferers of diabetes. Using her fame, she is a top fund-raiser and international chairman of the Juvenile Diabetes Research Foundation. Moore herself almost lost her vision and a limb to the disease. In May 2011, Mary Tyler Moore went through elective brain surgery to remove a benign meningioma. She's a devoted advocate for animal rights and an iconic figure of our culture. In front of Macy's in Minneapolis is a statue of fictional character Mary Richards throwing her tam into the air—frozen for generations who never heard of or watched her show to ask, "Who was Mary Tyler Moore?" That's pretty cool for an old lady.

People over thirty were considered old by the youth culture. Sure funny lady Fannie Flagg was a fixture on game shows, and impressionist Marilyn Michaels was racking up the voice count weekly on ABC's short-lived *Kopycats*. Bordering on the line was comedic actress Madeline Kahn, delivering brilliance in *Young Frankenstein, Blazing Saddles,* and *What's Up, Doc?*, but the '70s represented a turning point for comedy. The country was rapidly moving away from formula banter entertainment and long-in-the-tooth variety. Not only did audience attendance escalate on the big screen with the introduction of popcorn-fare blockbusters provided by maverick directors like Spielberg and Lucas, but TV filtered in younger and younger comedic personalities. Actresses such as the bubbly Karen Valentine (*Room 222*) and the even bubblier Sally Struthers (*All in the Family*) were driving up the ratings for their respective shows. Appealing to a younger demographic was in and Hollywood was preparing itself for more to come. Not that they staked out grade schools for talent, but they went to the next best place for unbridled, infantile behavior—the comedy clubs. There they found a gritty reality and uncensored imaginations. An explosion was about to take place.

CHAPTER 10

Ka-Boom

"I consider myself to be a pretty good judge of people . . . that's why I don't like any of them." —**Roseanne Barr**

The '80s saw a comedy boom, which benefited male as well as female performers. The country, as usual, was confused and laughter is always a sure-fire distraction. While Rhea Perlman and Shelley Long were serving up laughs on NBC's hit *Cheers,* Polly Holliday was telling her boss and customers to kiss her grits on *Alice* (which starred Linda Lavin), and Carol Kane mangled English on *Taxi,* new stars were created and self-titled sitcoms rolled off the assembly line. All a comedian had to do was show up on *The Tonight Show,* get a few nods and chuckles from Johnny Carson, and the next day their agent's phone was ringing off the hook. And for those fortunate enough to be invited to sit down and chat—your fortune was made.

ROSEANNE BARR

Roseanne Barr made her first *Tonight Show* appearance in 1985. The product of a Jewish family who was raised half-Jewish and half-Mormon in Salt Lake City in the 1950s, she was determined to keep their heritage a secret. At age sixteen, she was institutionalized for eight months following the effects of trauma to her brain after being hit by a car. At age eighteen, Barr ran off to Colorado to begin her career in stand-up comedy. Once she killed 'em on *The Tonight Show* and *Late Night with David Letterman,* Hollywood took notice. Roseanne taped her award-winning HBO comedy special, *The Roseanne Barr Show,* and turned down the role of Peg Bundy on *Married with Children* before landing her own sitcom on ABC in 1987. The part of Peg Bundy went to singer-songwriter Katey Sagal, with her scatter-brained daughter, Kelly, played by Christina Applegate.

Roseanne, based on her "domestic goddess" stage persona, was an immediate hit, but the star wasn't happy. Seems writer Matt Williams was getting credit as the show's creator and ABC had to decide if it was going to be Williams or Barr. Matt was given his walking papers after thirteen episodes. During the series's highly successful nine-season run, Barr divorced first husband and father to their three children, former motel clerk Bill Pentland; married fellow comedian and one-time opening act Tom Arnold four days later; sang the "Star Spangled Banner" off-key with a finale of spitting and crotch grabbing at the start of a Padres–Reds game (at the urging of baseball officials to make it funny and to the disgust of former president George H. W. Bush, who failed to see the humor); became the first female comedienne to host the MTV Video Music Awards; released her bestselling autobiography; made her film debut in *She Devil* to critical acclaim; divorced fellow comedian Tom Arnold (who, it was said, tried to use her for his own purposes); married personal security guard Ben Thomas; gave birth to her fourth child; and became the second highest-paid female performer ($40,000,000) behind Oprah Winfrey.

Roseanne has delved into every medium. Besides her successful sitcom, where she introduced gay characters at the urging of her own lesbian sister and gay brother, she appeared in *The Wizard of Oz* at Madison Square Garden as the Wicked Witch of the West. She had a talk show for two seasons and did an animated voice-over for the feature-length film *Home on the Range.* Her cooking show and reality show were cut short by a hysterectomy, but once recovered, Roseanne

Hrosvitha.

Sophie Tucker.

May Irwin.

Fanny Brice: "My Man".

Mae West.

Sandra Bernhard.

Thea Vidale and Jentle Phoenix.

Miss Laura Hayes and Lawanda Page on the set of *Martin*

Mo'Nique and Vanessa Fraction.

Sarah Silverman and Miss Laura Hayes.

Micki, Rodney Perry, Kym Whitley, Simply Cookie (in front),
and Darryl and Tuezdae Littleton.

Luenell and Paul Mooney.

Chelsea Handler and Loni Love.

The Queens of Comedy on *The Mo'Nique Show*. Left to Right: Miss Laura Hayes, Adele Givens, Sommore and Mo'Nique.

Tia and Tamara Mowry with fan Darina Littleton and friend.

B-Phlat and Lisa Lampanelli.

Queen Aisha, B-Phlat, Dana Austin, and Sherri Shepherd.

Melanie Carmacho, Robin Montague, Sylvia Traymoore, and two dudes.

Tiffany Haddish, Lady Roz G, Joyelle Johnson, Dominique, and Vanessa Fraction.

The Hot & Sexy Mamitas. Left to right: Ludo Vika, Sully Diaz, Marilyn Martinez, Lydia Nicole, and Dyana Ortelli.

Sheryl Underwood and Honest John.

went on a world tour doing stand-up, released a children's DVD, cranked out another HBO comedy special, divorced Ben Thomas, and, in 2008, began co-hosting a weekly radio show with new man friend Johnny Argent. She authored a bestselling book and moved with Argent to a macadamia-nut farm on the Big Island in Hawaii, where she shoots her reality show, *Roseanne's Nuts.*

RITA RUDNER

Rita Rudner got her big break on *The Tonight Show* in 1988. Laid-back and unassuming, the comedienne with the retiring sense of humor was, not surprisingly, born in the retirement capital of Miami, Florida. Starting in show biz as a dancer, Rudner appeared in several Broadway productions before turning to stand-up comedy at age twenty-five after noticing there were more female dancers than female comics. It wasn't long before she'd built a fan base and found her niche with an act based on domestic observations.

"My husband gave me a necklace. It's fake. I requested fake. Maybe I'm paranoid, but in this day and age, I don't want something around my neck that's worth more than my head."

"If you want to break up with a man, tell him, 'I love you. I want to marry you. I want to have your children. I want us to grow old together and be with each other forever.' Sometimes they leave skid marks."

On mothering: *"To me, life is tough enough without having someone kick you from the inside."*

Though she was recognized as one of the top comediennes of her generation, sitcom stardom eluded her, as did a sitcom. She shot half a dozen pilots, but none scored a bull's-eye. Rita's more known for her HBO comedy specials, *Rita Rudner: Born to Be Mild* and *Rita Rudner: Married Without Children.*

She's co-written several screenplays with husband, Martin
Bergman, one being *Peter's Friends* co-starring Kenneth
Branagh and Emma Thompson; she's also authored a
bestselling book and two novels, scribed a play, and after a
decade of stand-up success and peer envy, took her act to Las
Vegas and found the queen–of-mild humor was embraced
by Sin City. Rita Rudner has performed exclusively in Vegas
since 2001, selling over a million tickets.

TRACEY ULLMAN

Tracey Ullman didn't have to do *The Tonight Show.* She
came over from England. The one-time hit-making punk
rocker was making a lot of noise in the UK with her comedy
on the BBC show *Kicking Up the Eighties.* So renowned
television producer James Brooks invited her over to do some
US telly. The result was *The Tracey Ullman Show* in 1987,
the first hit for the newly introduced FOX network. On it she
played any number of diverse characters and was completely
unrecognizable in prosthetics and makeup.

Besides *The Tracy Ullman Show* winning four Emmy
Awards, Ullman also introduced the world to *The Simpsons,*
featuring the female voices of Yeardley Smith as Lisa, Julie
Kavner as Marge, and Nancy Cartwright as Bart. When the
latter was spun off to become a social and cultural cornerstone,
Tracey sued for her share. While waiting, she did two cable
specials and another series, *Tracy Take s On . . .* , for HBO,
playing uncensored characters this time (and this one won
eight Emmys); she wrote a book based on the series, did a talk
show, established a clothing line, appeared in films, recorded
animated voice-overs, gave birth for the second time, became
a naturalized citizen of the US, and later took her new series,
Tracy Ullman's State of the Union, to rival network Showtime
after a fourteen-year relationship with HBO. She was almost
too busy to notice that after years in court, she received a
portion of *The Simpsons* merchandising—a portion that was
added to the rest of her enterprises and put her at the top of the

list of "Britain's Wealthiest Citizens" in 2006 at £75 million.

The comedy boom, like most booms, was great for those who were positioned properly. For the unimaginative decision makers, all these new faces and personalities the boom produced meant categories had to be implemented. Women had to fit into a certain group for the industry to "get" them and how they could be utilized. Comedienne Felicia Michaels recalls those days: "Not that I'm, y'know, the most beautiful girl, 'cause I'm not. However, I would go on auditions . . . I was always the ugliest girl at the pretty girl auditions or the prettiest girl at the goofy girl auditions."

The boom of the '80s fattened quite a few pockets. Of course there were the inevitable casualties. Some capitalized; others capitalized and imploded, like Brett Butler and her time bomb, *Grace Under Fire,* where drug abuse abused a network's goodwill.

BRETT BUTLER

The Alabama-born cocktail-waitress-turned-stand-up-comedienne had the brass ring clenched firmly in her teeth when the pull of drugs yanked it out. From 1993 to 1998, Butler had one of the top performing shows on network television. Then she found herself dismissed after a series of erratic episodes off-camera. Chances had been many and excuses were worn out. ABC made sure *Grace Under Fire* became Grace fired: production halted; cast and crew were issued final checks. The party was over. Butler went back to life on the stage and living on a farm.

Society takes a dim view of such behavior. The average citizen and taxpayer work for a living. When they hear about the amounts of money celebrities make, it makes them want to puke. Most will never see that performer's weekly salary in five years, and surely not in a lump. So when a star blows it, there's scant sympathy for the blower. A shaking of heads and a "tsk, tsk" is pretty much the reaction, and then it's back to living lives. There'll be no marching in the street with placards to make a fallen star ascend again. If regular people have to suffer the consequences of their actions, then so should a spoiled TV actress who didn't know when she had it good. That's just human nature. That's why as wanton as the Brett Butler chapter was, she definitely was not the first, nor will she likely be the last, to squander a plum situation so publicly and have to deal with the backlash.

SUZANNE SOMERS

In 1982, Suzanne Somers, who gained fame as one-third of the ABC hit sitcom *Three's Company*, was fired after the fifth season for wanting more money than the producers were willing to pay. Somers's husband/business manager, Alan Hamel (who was married when they met and following a three-year affair got a divorce and married Somers), refused to budge from his demand of an increase from $30,000 to $150,000 per episode and 10 percent of the show's profits. Instead, while Somers made lame excuses to miss episodes during the bargaining process, Hamel negotiated a deal with rival CBS for *The Suzanne Somers Show,* so strongly did he feel that he was holding all the cards. The game went bad when their lawsuit against ABC for $2 million was basically thrown back in their faces with a win of only $30,000 for the one missed episode. Then CBS had a changing of the guard in upper management and the new crew passed on Somers's show. Her claim that her reputation in show business had been damaged by the ordeal was an understatement. It took a *Playboy* magazine nude spread (from old photos before she was famous) and a short-lived syndicated show (*She's the Sheriff*), but Somers made a comeback in *Step by Step,* which ran for seven seasons; she also sold trinkets on a shopping network, hawked an exercise device for thighs, and wrote books about herself (two autobiographies) and self-improvement.

SANDRA BERNHARD

Stand-up comedienne Sandra Bernhard was not as public with her controversy, but was just as slicing with her comments. While doing promotion for PlushGlass lip gloss, Bernhard referred to anyone who had a problem with her as a spokesperson as a "little freaked out, intimidated, frightened, right-wing Republican, thin-lipped bitch." That line was edited out of the commercial, one of a number of things that she did got edited. Outspokenness was her stock and trade when she first got noticed at Hollywood's Comedy Store. It wasn't long before she was plucked up by comedian Paul Mooney to be a regular on NBC's *The Richard Pryor Show.* The show itself only lasted four episodes, but Bernhard made an impression. She got her big break when director Martin Scorsese cast her as a crazed celebrity stalker in his film *The King of Comedy* with Robert De Niro and comedienne lover Jerry Lewis. She won the National Society of Film Critics Award for Best Supporting Actress.

Sandra Bernhard went back to the stage. She mounted a one-woman show, titled *I'm Your Woman,* in 1985 and released an accompanying album. In 1988, she staged another one-woman show—*Without You I'm Nothing, with You I'm Not Much Better.* It was turned into a film in 1990 and a double album. It was alluded to on *Late Night with David Letterman* that Sandra and Madonna were lesbian lovers. That rumor picked up steam in 1991 when Bernhard became a recurring character on *Roseanne,* playing the role of Nancy Bartlett, an open lesbian (the first on American television). In 1992, she did a nude pictorial in *Playboy;* did a bevy of guest-starring roles on TV; returned to Broadway with her show, *I'm Still Here . . . Damn It!,* and gave birth to her daughter, Cicely Yasin Bernhard. Sandra has released several albums where she mixes comedy with her performances of pop, jazz, and blues tunes.

ELAYNE BOOSLER

If it wasn't for the only daughter of a Russian acrobat father and a Romanian ballerina mother, comediennes on cable might still be a "what if." Brooklyn-born Elayne Boosler worked at the door of the Improv in New York for three years before comedian Andy Kaufman told her she should be on the stage and not at the door. Kaufman took her in as a girlfriend and protégé and schooled her in the ins and outs of comedy. Before long she was wrecking stages and got her own Showtime hour-long special in 1986. She had to finance it herself due to executive ignorance and fear in a woman doing stand-up for that long. However, once the reviews came out, they proclaimed Boosler's outing a success, including praise from *People* magazine, which gave it an "A."

The industry was so mesmerized that rival cable network HBO came out with its own specials for women. She was red-hot until an off-the-cuff remark put the brakes on her career. While appearing on CNN's *Crossfire,* Boosler said Mother Theresa was a hypocrite for not bringing birth control to Calcutta. The hosts were visibly panicked and cut to a commercial break. The industry also panicked and cut the knees off of Boosler's rapidly ascending career. She continued to work, but the air had definitely been let out of the balloon.

Comedy remained a hard navigation for comediennes, but at least they were getting bigger and better shots. Whether they struck out or not, they were finally getting to the plate in the big game. Many came to the forefront—including comediennes such as Paula Poundstone, Judy Tenuta, Jenny Jones, Bonnie Hunt, Shelley Pryor, Etta Mae, Geri Jewell, Diane Nichols, Caroline Rhea, Wendy Leiberman, and Stephanie Hodge—and have remained active in front and behind the scenes.

CHAPTER 11

Can They Talk?

"I don't look like Halle Berry. But chances are, she's going to end up looking like me." —**Whoopi Goldberg**

Besides a mainstream comedy boom, the '80s gave us cable networks ONTV and Select, video games by Atari, and musical groups with big hair wearing tight pants. There were jiggle shows, goofy sitcoms, lawyer dramas, funny Bette Midler movies, and unemployed traffic controllers. And then there was Joan Rivers.

JOAN RIVERS

She had to compete against all of that. No problem. She'd cut her comedy teeth in Chicago's Second City and comedy clubs in New York's Greenwich Village. As Johnny Carson's go-to guest host, the raspy voiced comedienne who'd been plugging away since the '60s was finally getting some serious attention. So much so that in 1986, the newly christened FOX network beckoned Rivers over to do her own late-night talk show.

Being a pioneer means sacrifice. Not only did Rivers's show die a rancid death, after attempting to fire husband,

Edgar Rosenberg (who was the producer), FOX ended up firing them both. Three months later, Rosenberg was found dead from an apparent suicide. Joan blamed FOX. Several years later, she found success on a daytime talk show. She also got daughter Melissa in on the act by co-hosting the E! Entertainment network's Golden Globes pre-show and Academy Awards pre-show and ripping celebrities a new one.

"I like people that don't really give a damn and just say whatever. Sometimes I wish I had balls like that, but I'm too scared to hurt people's feelings." —Nikki Carr

Joan Alexandra Molinsky from Brooklyn didn't have time to care about other people's feelings. She was too busy trying to get ahead. After graduating from Barnard College with a bachelor of arts degree in English literature and anthropology, she worked a number of diverse jobs: tour guide at Rockefeller Center, writer/proofreader at an ad agency, and fashion consultant.

Rivers began her show biz career in the theater and New York comedy clubs and landed on *The Tonight Show* hosted by Jack Paar. She was a gag writer for *Candid Camera,* as well as a plant to sucker participants into doing wacky things. It was during the '60s that she made her first foray into the talk-show format with a daytime talk show of her own. Her first guest was Johnny Carson. She also released two comedy albums during this decade.

The 1970s saw a Rivers expansion. She appeared on variety shows (*The Carol Burnett Show*), participated in children's programming (*The Electric Company*), and did game shows (*Hollywood Squares*). She wrote the Stockard Channing movie comedy *The Girl Most Likely To . . .* and wrote and directed the Billy Crystal film *Rabbit Test.* She also introduced herself to Las Vegas audiences as singer Helen Reddy's opening act.

By the '80s, Rivers was headlining Vegas. She took her growing cache and wrote a bestselling humor book, *The Life and Hard Times of Heidi Abramowitz.* Her popularity was such that she found herself initiating a lawsuit against drag queen Frank Marino for doing her stand-up material as part of his impersonation of her. This was also the decade she became estranged from longtime friend and mentor Carson after jumping over to FOX and directly challenging him for viewers and precious ratings. Once that whirlwind of missteps and tragedy subsided, Joan stepped back into the daytime talk-show arena with *The Joan Rivers Show* and got an Emmy and a five-year run for her efforts.

The only thing that was getting more attention than Joan Rivers's own biting self-deprecating wit was her multiple plastic surgeries. She's never shied away from the fact that she's had some work done, having popped up on three episodes of *Nip/Tuck* playing herself and as a vagina that's had too much plastic surgery in the animated adult show *Drawn Together*.

The new millennium found business-savvy Rivers being omnipresent. She had an $8 million deal to do TV Guide's red-carpet show, leaving E! holding considerably less. She had a line of baubles called, what else, The Joan Rivers Collection being hawked on the QVC shopping network. She was one in only four Americans invited to Prince Charles's wedding and won Donald Trump's NBC reality show hit, *The Celebrity Apprentice*. Joan Rivers is no mere comedienne. She's a comedy factory.

WHOOPI GOLDBERG

Another comedienne pulling the Renaissance routine burst upon the scene in a one-woman show she created, entitled *The Spook Show*. Famed director Mike Nichols took it to Broadway, and the artist who could do so many funny characters ruled the town.

"I remember when she first did her one-woman show. She was crazy in that. It was way in the beginning when stand-up was different and she puts on this one-woman show doing all these characters. It was remarkable." —Sara Contreras

Caryn Elaine Johnson, later known as Whoopi Goldberg, was then cast as Celie in Alice Walker's *The Color Purple,* directed by Steven Spielberg, and in 1985, became a household name. From there Whoopi was making plenty. Besides film, Goldberg had her own NBC sitcom and a late-night talk show. She co-produced the popular game show *The Hollywood Squares,* wrote books, produced plays on Broadway, did voice-overs in classic cartoons (*Lion King* and *Toy Story*), co-founded Comic Relief, was the first black female to host the Academy Awards, and co-hosted the morning gabfest *The View.* By the way, did I mention she won an Oscar (for *Ghost*), making her the first African American stand-up comedienne to receive the award?

"I auditioned for a great movie. They were looking for an unknown actress. The movie was called Ghost. *I went to the casting director, then to the director, the writer—they were absolutely amazed. The writer said this is who I saw when I was writing the script. This is it! We wanted an unknown and she's perfect. They sent me paperwork to be in that movie. And then Whoopi Goldberg decided she wanted that part. It was taken away from me. I had been on a high from the moment I got to Los Angeles. My little bubble popped really hard. I was back to being a comic again."* —Jedda Jones

Goldberg understood the business she was in and how to manipulate it to her benefit, all the way down to her name change. Whoopi was a nickname associated with her for her ability to release pressure from an individual (with laughter), similar to whoopee cushions. However, she adopted the name Goldberg because her mother told her Johnson wasn't Jewish enough to make her a star. And not only did she become that, one year she was recognized as the highest paid actress of all time. Her output was tremendous by any measure. After winning the Academy Award in 1990 for *Ghost,* Goldberg has appeared in no less than three films a year, every year, with a high count of seven motion pictures in 1998. She did this for twenty straight years. Talk about a role model. She was also generous, even though she'd try to do things without much fanfare.

"Took the Ghost *job away from me, but she also gave me an opportunity. She introduced me as her protégé a few years later and gave me an HBO comedy special, and she felt like she was trying to make it up to me. She did feel bad about taking that part from me and she did try to give me something in exchange." —*Jedda Jones

Race and gender were minor obstacles in her approach. From the very beginning, Goldberg set her sights on what was normally not considered traditional black casting. This sprung from one of her first experiences seeing this practice. While watching *Star Trek* as a youth, she called out to her mother that there was a black woman on TV who was not a maid. Nichelle Nichols's portrayal of Uhura on the *Starship Enterprise* sparked in Goldberg the desire to be all she could be. She even auditioned for the lead in the film *The Princess Bride*, a role that requested a blond-haired, blue-eyed, single white female. She didn't get the part, but not due to lack of trying. When she couldn't win parts meant for men, she played men in parts (*The Associate* in 1996). And a white man at that.

"One of the few black female comedians that came out that was able to talk about controversial issues and made people very uncomfortable while they were relaxing."
—Edwonda White

Goldberg was also no stranger to controversy. Often criticized by the African American community for dating out of her race, Goldberg married director of photography David Claessen and divorced soon after the failure of one of her contracted films, *The Telephone*. That was her second marriage. Her first lasted six years; her third held on for one.

In 1995, she convinced boyfriend Ted Danson to don blackface at a Friar's Club event that got publicized and scrutinized, and in 2004 she lost her Slim-Fast endorsement after telling an off-colored joke about sitting president George W. Bush. She's been a vocal proponent of whatever she chose to be vocal about as co-host of *The View* and has never lost sight of her power in the medium. She's there to entertain, to be Whoopi— and she's all that.

She replaced Rosie O'Donnell on *The View* in 2007 with the support of O'Donnell herself via her popular blog. Goldberg's debut got one million less viewers than O'Donnell's debut ratings, but after two weeks, Whoopi saw a 7 percent increase from the previous season. She came out of the box saying that NFL quarterback Michael Vick's dogfighting was "part of his cultural upbringing" and "not all that unusual" in parts of the South. That was pretty controversial because most of the country was solidly against Vick and wanted to hear no excuses, based in fact or not. He'd been convicted of animal cruelty and served a twenty-three-month sentence for running a dogfighting ring in which the losing dogs were killed as punishment for being weak. Goldberg repeatedly stated she didn't condone what Vick did, but that's not the stuff that makes the press, so oh well.

Whoopi took on comedic celebrities. After comedienne Kathy Griffin called Senator Scott Brown's daughters "prostitutes," Goldberg said that if anyone insulted her daughter like that, "I would beat their ass." Don't look so shocked. You hired Whoopi Goldberg. As a veteran comedienne, she knew who she was and who she was going to be to that audience. As one of the few entertainers to have won an Oscar, a Tony, an Emmy, and a Grammy, she knew her power and where things stood historically. The woman knew the score and how to keep it.

JOY BEHAR

Whoopi Goldberg found a formidable counterpart on *The View*. Born Josephina Victoria "Joy" Occhiuto, Joy Behar was also a controversial lightning rod, from her opinions about Communions at the Catholic Church ("The priests were all drunk, don't you remember?") to her attitude about then-defense secretary Donald Rumsfeld ("Hitler-like"). She called Rachel Uchitel "a hooker" on air and walked off the set with Goldberg after disagreeing with remarks made by guest Bill O'Reilly. Behar kept jaws dropping and executives in need of antacids. The bawdy Italian stand-up kept her teeth away from her tongue to avoid ever biting it.

Behar gained notoriety on the New York comedy circuit and as a radio talk-show host on station WABC. She joined the panel on *The View* in 1997, keeping comedy in the forefront by hosting a segment called "Joy's Comedy Corner," where she presents new unknown comedians to the mass audience. The comedy community applauded her for such efforts. It was her show colleagues she often had problems with, like the time Star Jones was elaborating via conference call about an operation she'd just undergone and Behar cut her off with, "Okay, Star. That's enough about you. On to us. Bye. Keep your [breasts] perky!" Without missing a beat, Jones called Behar a bitch.

All name calling aside, Behar's no average bitch. She holds a bachelor of arts degree in sociology and a master of arts degree in English education. Joy taught English in the late 1960s and early 1970s at Lindenhurst High School and is a member of the Delta Zeta sorority. She's been married twice, first to Joe Behar in a sixteen-year union that produced a daughter, and second after a long relationship to Steve Janowitz. The woman has also appeared in films and theater and authored two books, one a collection of humorous essays and stories called *Joy Shtick—Or What Is the Existential Vacuum and Does It Come with Attachments?* and the other a children's book called *Sheetzucacapoopoo: My Kind of Dog*. Her own talk show ran on CNN HLN for over two years.

or not, eventually that's what a big-shot muckety-muck was going to ask you to do anyway. Why not cut to the chase?

Felicia Michaels looked at it this way: "I figured given my physical package, people in positions of power wouldn't hear what I was saying."

Michaels posed for *Playboy,* but she wasn't alone.

"Female comics were wanted for Playboy. *They didn't ask me." —*Thea Vidale

The 1990s also saw a boom of another sort. It was a black comedy boom. Once *Def Comedy Jam* made its debut on HBO, comedians of all shapes, sizes, and genders were sought to fill the public's insatiable demand for funny African Americans. The explosion couldn't be contained after cable got hold of the uncensored diatribes, but before Russell Simmons could unleash this phenomenon upon the world, the Wayans over at FOX had a thing or four to say about women in comedy: namely Kelli Coffer, Kim Coles, T'Keyah "Crystal" Keymah, and little sister Kim Wayans. These women were the heart and soul of *In Living Color,* a show that changed the face of televised comedy and launched more careers than NASA did shuttles.

Television and film studios clamored to make stars out of stage performers, some so new they dripped milk from behind their ears. Those ready for the challenge rose to the occasion. Simply Marvelous led the pack with a *Def Jam* appearance that galvanized and a HBO hour-long special that fans of the craft talked about for years. She was poised for a medium and industry push when tragedy showed up in the form of a sick relative and later a debilitating stroke.

Looking back, she had this to say about her promising career and HBO special: "I wasn't ready for that and the people at that time would die to do a HBO special. I wasn't prepared for that. I should've waited another year."

The trailblazer was one of the first females to do *Def Comedy Jam,* but has her reservations about that appearance as well.

"I met Russell Simmons at the Comedy Act Theater. He gave me his card and people asked me if I knew who that was. I said, 'No, who is he?' They said, 'That's Run DMC's brother.' When it was time for *Def Jam,* Russell had already bought my ticket and told me just to be there. No one had even told me about *Def Jam.* It was meant to be, but if I could do it all over again I would do it in a different way. I would change my nasty tongue. I would've done Christian comedy."

Simply had been a Comedy Act Theater regular and had maneuvered her way into making friends in comedy, like the legendary LaWanda Page.

"I was working at a customer service place in Oakland or San Francisco and I ran up on her name and I called her, which I wasn't supposed to do, and I asked her if she would listen to a tape of mine. She said, 'Yeah,' and invited me over to her house and I was just overwhelmed by just hearing her and talking to her."

The late Robin Harris was also an early fan of her unpredictable banter.

"This girl in the audience, she came up to me and said she didn't come to this show to be insulted. Well, first of all you, don't go to a comedy show if you don't want to be insulted because anything may come out of a comic's mouth. I gave her her money back and said if it hurt you that bad, you should leave. Robin came down to the Comedy Act Theater and laughed so hard he ran down the aisles in between the seats. I miss it a lot. I know I can't do it like I used to."

Gut-busting laughter was the theme of that era. Songstress Della Reese showed off her comedy chops in 1989's *Harlem Nights* when she went toe to toe with Eddie Murphy in an alley fight and knocked him off his feet and into a pile of trash cans with a wicked uppercut. She continued her hilarious ways in 1991 with Redd Foxx on the CBS show *Royal Family.* BeBe Drake and Roxanne Reese were slaying on *Martin* as Myra, Stan's girlfriend, and Marian, the local alcoholic, respectively. *Martin* leading lady Tisha Campbell (Gina) was doing films like *House Party* and *School Daze,* as well as going wanted to do stand-up comedy. She was like, 'Have you lost your mind? Well, somebody needs to go out there and get that baby and bring him (Myra's son) back to Chicago 'cause she done moved to LA and went Hollywood and now she wants to tell some knock-knock jokes.' My mama said, 'You got a good government job.' She said, 'Girl, you got a credit union. How you gonna give that up?' That was the support I got from my family."

The urban comedy boom put an exclamation point on the mainstream boom and breathed additional life into the public fixation with laughter. A flood of newness poured over the land and everybody who didn't have a comedy club opened theirs in bars, bowling alleys, and coffeehouses. It was time to get paid and all self-described comics worked. Women were in demand . . . to do comedy. Sheryl Underwood, Sherri Shepherd, Adele Givens, Ajai Sanders, Myra J, Phyllis, Yvonne Stickney, Luenell, Montanna Taylor, Jedda Jones (Ms. Dupre), Robin Montague, Yvette Wilson, Roxanne Reese, Wanda Smith, Miss Laura Hayes, Angela Means, Roz Brown, Lisa Holly, Kathy Westfield, Edwonda White, Tess, Olivia Arrington, Lady Roz, Queen Aisha, Kim Tavares, GiGi Bolden, Debra Terry, Chocolate, Sommore, Small Frie, Diane Corder, Hope Flood, Sandy Brown, Tasha Smith, Pat Brown, Melanie Comarcho, Dirty South, Debra Wilson, Coco, Kym Whitley, Leslie, Dominique, Retha Jones, Dana Point, Cookie, Karen Addison, Mo'Nique, Annie McKnight, Barbara Carlyle, Jus June, and a cavalcade of comediennes took their rightful place on those stages wherever they were to be found.

Road work was plentiful. It was a resurgence of the old chitlin circuit, with all the opportunities. In the heyday of the boom era, comedy was queen. Round-trip tickets (sometimes first class), airport pickup in limousines, enviable hotel accommodations in rooms you hated to leave, fruit baskets, food trays, and liquor at the venue, top dollar for your services, and unlimited adulation. If you weren't in front of a camera on a television or movie set—don't fret. The road would treat you right. Some hit it to gain a following—others for love of travel. Others still because it made more financial sense.

"Yes, my husband and I had the five-year plan. If my money kept moving on up, I could stand up, he saw that Mitzi, Bud, Bob, everybody was making money and comics were just happy to stand up for three minutes. He asked me where do comics have to go to make money (I started in '83). I said on the road. He told me to pack my bags. I've been a road dog ever since."
—Jus June

It was great, but similar to the chitlin circuit of old, the road offered danger as well. You had to keep your eyes open and watch your back.

"There was a time when, black comics especially, we had our own underground railroad. That's the only way I can say it. If comics got stranded in cities where other black comics were or cool white boys were, we would hook them up with the numbers and we would say, 'Look, if you here, you can go and stay with these people. Even my house was one of the houses you could stay at." —Thea Vidale

"Most of us are out by ourselves. We don't have entourages. You have to put your safety and business before anything. Just come in, handle your business, then be out." —B-Phlat

"There were some dangerous times. You know, coming out of a show and have some fans be walking along with you and all of a sudden say something like, 'You make a lot of money, don't you?' Uh, no, nigga, actually I don't."
—Miss Laura Hayes

"If I'm on the road and it's after a show and 'Hey, let's go to a bar,' I'm not going to do that. I stay with the people I know. When I'm done, I'm done. I go back to the hotel. I lock the door. I'm aware of my surroundings at all times. As a woman,

you have to be. I just don't have that approachable thing. Lesbians approach me more than men. I don't know what I'm giving off, but my daughter's gay. So I must've given it to her."
—Shayla Rivera

"I always took a guy with me, and a lot of time it would be an undercover cop or undercover security just for protection."
—Ajai Sanders

"I travel with a road manager if I'm going to be out for a long period of time. I make sure I don't do stupid stuff like a lot of women do. I'm not going to be alone with strange men. You never know what's going to happen."
—Edwonda White

I did ride in cars with comics I didn't know about, but this is a vouching-for system. It's show business. It was risky, plus I'm from D.C. I know how to fuck a nigga up." —Robin Montague

"I've always had that reputation that I don't take no stuff. They know I'm a collector of guns and weapons."
—Olivia Arrington

Another danger was narrow-minded club owners who hadn't gotten the memo that women were just as funny as men.

"There was one gig in New Jersey. When I got there, the club owner said, 'I told them don't send me no girls.' So he called the booker and said, 'I didn't want no girls.' So the booker calls another comic to come and take my spot. The comedian said, 'Well, who's there?' The booker said, 'Jedda.' The comedian said, 'That's bullshit. She can handle that room. I'm not going to take her job.' So the booker said, 'Deal with her or don't, but she's getting paid.' So the owner put me on first. I was actually booked as the feature. He goes up and says, 'They sent a girl. I don't know what she's going to do and her name is . . . what's your name? Jedda Jones.' And he puts the microphone

*on the floor. So I had to pick the microphone up off the floor.
I was so angry, I killed that room for revenge. Then he falls in
love with me. He kept saying, 'Send Jedda back.' So now every
time I go to his club, I'm headlining. He's buying me bottles of
champagne. He's buying me jewelry."* —Jedda Jones

Comediennes became bookers and changed some of the
outdated methods—not just shows in the appliance store after
hours either, but also overseas military tours and major clubs.

*"I made it one of my priorities to always book a lot of females
out here on the road because it was difficult to get jobs as a
female. I wasn't really worried about what the guys thought
about it, but my thing was I'm'a book who's funny and whose
chemistry will work together. I pay them the same thing I pay
the men. You know, you went and did a gig, maybe even more
time or the same time as the guy, and you get way less, but you
don't know that 'til you already did it."* —Olivia Arrington

In many cases the rewards for the performers were
immeasurable.

*"Getting to be of service and going to perform for the
troops, who are thanking you for coming, and you just feel so
humbled right away because you're so grateful for them."*
—Jentle Phoenix

The road kept non-traceable money in the pockets of
comediennes, but to make the money that's made while you're
asleep—annuity cash; the gift that keeps on giving—you
needed true media exposure. Not the guest-starring spots on
stand-up shows where the credits say you played yourself.
No TV—starring or sidekick. Film—make an impression; be
memorable. That's how to keep the checks rolling in and the
work steadily coming. Make a big enough name for yourself,
and then the road paid even better money than the average
well-paid humorist was pulling down.

WANDA SYKES

One of the chief beneficiaries of this era was Wanda Sykes. She started her stand-up career at a Coors Light Super Talent Showcase in Washington, DC, in 1987. So by 1992, when the comedy boom was at its peak, she moved to New York, got her stand-up chops tightened, and opened for Chris Rock at Caroline's. From there, the former military brat and NSA procurement officer wrote for Rock's show, earning an Emmy for the gig in 1999. Other opportunities soon followed. Her first major film was the Eddie Murphy Murphyfest *Nutty Professor II: The Klumps,* followed by Rock's *Down to Earth* and *Pootie Tang,* the movie version of the character made popular on *The Chris Rock Show* by comedian Lance Caruthers.

Television was Wanda's friend as well. In 2003, she got her own show on FOX, entitled *Wanda at Large.* The show didn't last long, but Sykes definitely made an impression, and before long she developed a budding relationship with Comedy Central. That same year she did their hour-long special *Tongue Untied,* got ranked number 70 on Comedy Central's list of the 100 greatest all-time stand-ups, hosted their comedian showcase, *Premium Blend,* and voiced the character of Gladys on the puppet show *Crank Yankers;* she also starred in another short-lived show, *Wanda Does It.* Not to be outdone, HBO got into the Wanda Sykes business and had her serve as correspondent for their program *Inside the NFL.*

In 2004, Sykes put pen to paper and wrote her first book, *Yeah, I Said It,* and then it was back in front of the cameras. She shot the films *Mother-in-Law* with screen legend Jane Fonda. In 2006, she was everywhere, or at least in eight projects, either as a voice (*Over the Hedge* and *Barnyard*) or in theaters (*My Super Ex-Girlfriend* and *Clerks II*) as well as landing the role of Barbara Baran, Julia Louis Dreyfus's friend in the CBS sitcom *The New Adventures of Old Christine.*

Wanda had comedy specials, her own talk show, and a social conscience. In November 2008, she came out of the closet and announced she was a lesbian while at a same-sex rally in Las Vegas. She had long been a strong advocate of same-sex marriage (despite her having been married to record producer Dave Hall from 1991 to 1998), but once she made her sexuality known, she put more effort into her activism. Wanda hosted events for GLAAD, participated in fund-raisers, and did commercials for GLSEN to change the mindset of youths about saying "That's so gay" as a negative and instead saying, "That's so bad."

Unlike many closeted celebrities, none of this seemed to injure her career. She married her wife, Alex, who gave birth to twins in April 2009. In May of the same year, Sykes became the first African American female, and its first openly LGBT person, to serve as a featured entertainer for the annual White House Correspondents' Association dinner. At this event, she said she hoped conservative radio talk show host Rush Limbaugh's kidney failed, in response to Limbaugh saying he hoped newly elected African American president Barack Obama failed. This didn't hurt her either. Wanda continued to shoot comedy specials, garner awards, and work in mainstream television and motion pictures. So maybe America was growing up—just maybe.

Wanda Sykes was not the only one to take advantage of the timing of the urban comedy boom. Several veteran performers were slightly ahead of the curve. One of them was known for just that—her curves, along with her wild assortment of wigs, many of the spiked variety. She was big in size and personality and she had the world on a string. Her name was Thea.

"That's the only woman on the road I feel safe with."
—Aida Rodriguez

THEA VIDALE

L ike Wanda Sykes, Thea Vidale cut her teeth in comedy clubs in Washington DC and New York. She got her break in 1989, when Vidale appeared in the cable comedy special *Rodney Dangerfield: Opening Night at Rodney's Place* on HBO.

She said of her experiences, "When I was a younger woman, it was just blatant misogyny out there. I got to deal with sexist behavior from white, black, and Latino comics, and I got to deal with the fact you don't want a woman to be funnier than you."

She was a woman in the world of men, and she measured up to the likes of Tim Allen, Jeff Foxworthy, and Sam Kinison handily.

"I featured for Tim Allen, Brad Garrett, Jeff Foxworthy— you name them, I featured for them. Hell, they're the reason I got to be a headliner. They would all ask the same question, 'Why aren't you headlining?' I'd say, 'I think its 'cause you in the way.'"

Sometimes featuring can be a pain, especially if you're a woman dealing with a lower-level headliner.

"My husband used to beat me, and after he and I separated I didn't want a man to touch me, so when men tried to, I'd punch 'em. I didn't give a fuck. I carried a pistol. I carried a .357 Magnum. Beulah. Beulah. I had a comic try to tell me . . . see, back in the day, the feature act had to go to the airport, if you were doing a road tour, and pick up the headliner, and I picked up Todd (Glass). He had a baggie full of coke. I'll never forget this, and oh, he was just a poppin' off—just poppin' off. He told me, he said, 'You had to pick me up,' and I said, 'Let me tell you something. If I want you out this car, you'd get out this car. He said, 'How you gonna make me get out this car?' This is the arrogance and mindset of white, straight, male headliners. You gonna tell me in my shit what I have to do. I told him me and Beulah would make you get out this car. He said, 'Who is Beulah?' I pulled out that .357 Magnum. He said, 'Oh my God.' I said, 'Yeah, this is Beulah and you will get out. He said, 'Just put the gun away.' I said, 'Just so we clear on what the fuck the dealio is; this way we real clear about who's running what up in this bitch. Make no mistakes.'"

Soon she was headlining clubs across the country and making guest appearances on every available televised stand-up show and sitcom that wanted laughter in big doses on the menu. Thea appeared on *Ellen, The Wayans Bros, The Drew Carey Show,* and *My Wife and Kids.* Off-camera she was opinionated and some say slightly insensitive. Regardless, Thea got her own show bearing her own name on ABC. This was a first for an African American female. The show, *Thea,* lasted one season, and Vidale was back on the road, where her onstage style was in your face and to the point.

An advocate for gay rights, Thea made her first appearance for GLBT in 1999. It was the Philadelphia GLBT Pride Fest with comic Etta May. The city's mayor officially named the day "Thea Vidale Day and Etta May Day. Vidale went on to work events for the Adult Film Industry (the AVN Awards) and perform as an WWE wrestler as Shelton Benjamin's mother. This latter was mock, but when Vidale experienced real-life heart problems, her character was written out of the charade. She acknowledged things got tough for a while professionally, from the industry and peers alike.

"I heard something that was said, Mike Epps said about me. He was looking for a female comic and he said, 'Ain't nobody looking for her.' He didn't say I wasn't funny. He dismissed me. And it's like, y'know I want to tell Mike to his face, 'What makes you other than your money? Every movie that you've played in you played the same person. Don't act like you are Othello. Don't do that! What gives you the right to dismiss me? You were looking for a woman. I asked my agent to submit me. You picked [another comedienne]. I ain't seen [her] on shit. I'm not mad at who you picked. I just question you dismissing me as if I'm nobody.'"

Vidale discovered, as did many who came before her, that ageism is also a negative for a black comedienne.

"I think the older you get, they try to discredit you unless you're a white male. White men get to be funny for a long time. Black men get to be funny. For some reason, women, as we get older, it seems they don't want to hear what we have to say. I got a lot of shit to say."

Show business has always been a revolving door, with the old guard outgoing as the public welcomes the new in. There's always the hope they would bring some form of innovation—a first. The boom was good for providing "firsts" as the powers that be scrambled, looking for the next way to exploit an audience thirsty for the new. Asia provided the solution they sought. Or at least a sitcom centered round an Asian.

MARGARET CHO

According to Hollywood lore, Margaret Cho was the first comedienne of Asian descent to star in her own sitcom, *All American Girl,* on ABC in 1994. That's if you don't count *Mr. T and Tina* two decades previously, on ABC as well. The latter show aired for five episodes in the fall of 1976 and starred Pat Morita. It was a spin-off of *Welcome Back, Kotter,* with Morita (of *Karate Kid* and *Happy Days,* where he played Arnold Takahashi) as a Japanese inventor living with a young American played by Susan Blanchard.

The distinction Cho holds is being the first Asian comedienne with her own sitcom. A major achievement considering Cho's culture looks down on such displays of foolishness. Yet she was pointed in that direction as soon as Mom met Dad. Born in the late '60s, Cho was raised in San Francisco. Her father wrote joke books and owned a bookstore. There was a comedy club nearby, and Margaret developed her act around the old hippies, drag queens, drug heads, and immigrants in the area. After working universities for years, she got a break with a role on *The Golden Girls* spin-off, *The Golden Palace,* then as Jerry Seinfeld's opening act.

In a profession dominated by men and few Asians of any gender, Margaret got noticed. ABC took her act and churned out *All American Girl.* For Cho, it was more like All American Nightmare. The producers kept tweaking the premise of the show, from Cho living with her parents in the house to living in their basement to moving out and living with three men— without explanation. They fired cast members and attempted to find ways to spin-off other shows from a show that obviously wasn't working itself. They didn't like her weight and round face, so she starved herself in an effort to appear like the Margaret Cho they had in mind, the fictionalized version. The result was major kidney problems for the real version. They told her she wasn't Asian enough and brought in an Asian consultant to Asian her up. That failed, so they fired the Asian cast and moved her in with white guys, then told her she was too Asian. All this led to the show being canceled after one season and Margaret Cho (the real life one) becoming an alcoholic and drug addict. If those producers had had their way, she would've committed hari-kari during Sweeps Week.

It took Cho awhile to pull out of her depression and addictions and resume comedy work. The show was not the only downer. She had never met with acceptance in the Korean community for her choice of profession. She was looked down upon, and this naturally didn't help when her shot at worldwide success fizzled.

Asian comedienne Rosie Tran knows the feeling of cultural rejection. "Sometimes I'll do a show and I'm the only Asian girl on the show and I really stand out. But more with other Asians. They're a little bit more judgmental because I'm kind of representing to them. So sometimes it's like a backlash from my own people."

Cho's romantic relationships (one with Quentin Tarantino) had also run their courses, and in a need for acceptance anywhere, Cho fell in and out of beds. Her act suffered so bad after cancelation, she was famously booed offstage in 1995 by over 800 college students. It wasn't until Margaret hit bottom that she rediscovered her comedic voice. She wrote a one-woman show, *I'm the One That I Want,* chronicling her insecurities over weight and beauty, turned it into her first book of the same title (her second was *I Have Chosen to Stay and Fight* in 2005). Then she filmed that concert material and released it as a film in 2000. She appeared in major motion pictures (*Face/Off* with John Travolta and *17 Again* with Matthew Perry), had her own reality show/sitcom on VH1 called *The Cho Show,* wrote and starred in the 2004 film *Bam*

Bam and Celeste, competed on *Dancing with the Stars,* and toured the world with her one-woman show and stand-up routine, which was filled with social, racial, and biting political humor (upon hearing 2008 presidential candidate John McCain chose Alaska governor Sarah Palin as his running mate, Cho said, "I think [Palin] is the worst thing to happen to America since 9/11").

Margaret Cho tested her talents in a number of areas and dived in headfirst on all. In 2002, she started her own clothing line, but the company eventually went belly up. When she got into belly dancing, she came out with a line of belly-dancing belts and accessories and sold them on her website. She became such a tattoo enthusiast that she tattooed roughly 15 percent of her body. Cho's done concert films, TV guest-starring roles, and music videos; she also recorded songs. She was such an advocate of gay and lesbian causes that Cho was deputized in California and performed same-sex marriages. Her own bi-sexuality was common knowledge, while she's maintained what she calls a conventional marriage with artist Al Ridenour since 2003. The reality—there's nothing conventional about Margaret Cho. Thank Buddha.

The era also proved that sometimes a proven formula needs to be tweaked. When both Selma Diamond and Florence Halop passed away from lung cancer, the producers for the NBC sitcom *Night Court* switched gears. They abandoned the notion of recasting with another older white character actress and hired a younger black comedienne. The result: a strong female persona emerged that influenced how females are portrayed in comedy forever—courtesy of stand-up veteran Marsha Warfield.

MARSHA WARFIELD

Marsha Warfield came from a broken home that got fixed. Not long after her younger sister, Cassandra, was born, her father left the family. Marsha's mother got another one. Her stepfather was employed as a computer operator for the city's library system while her mother worked at the telephone company. So the family was middle class and comfortable at home. School was another matter. Warfield was a lackadaisical student, preferring to sit in the back of the class and crack jokes about the teacher and classmates. Humor came natural for the shy girl and she was funny. So after graduating and spending a short period working at the phone company and an equally short period in a marriage, she tried her hand at stand-up comedy at the insistence of her close friend Evelyn. That night at Tom Dreesen's open mike changed her life profoundly.

Warfield got her break when comedian and Richard Pryor collaborator Paul Mooney picked her for *The Richard Pryor Show* in 1977. She was blunt, sexy, and uncompromising. The powerhouse comedienne had made her mark on the stand-up-comedy circuit, and Mooney knew she'd be equal to the task of writing and performing with the red-hot Pryor. At that time, Pryor was the comedy god. Or as she once said, "God takes second billing as far as Richard was concerned." So there were high expectations. She didn't disappoint, as Warfield and the rest of the cast made an indelible impression in the four short episodes they had on network television. However, the failure of the show left her depressed with thoughts of quitting comedy. That was until she won the prestigious San Francisco National Stand-Up Comedy Competition in '79.

Like many traveling performers, Warfield enjoyed the perks, but also acknowledged the downside of life on the road and being in comedy, period. This is what she told the *Chicago Tribune:* "I don't like traveling because I never get to see anything and I don't get to go anywhere. In every city, I know how to get from the airport to the hotel, from the hotel to the nightclub, and that's it. When I do get time off, I'm usually writing, working on my act and getting ready for the show." She added, "There are always problems and you get upset, but you do all of it to get back to the stage. So if it's a little inconvenient, I have to deal with it because I have to perform."

She told the *Herald de Paris:* "Performing is asking people you don't know to give you a hug—and it's devastating if they don't like you. Comedy," she says, is "almost like a fix" to her and she has little to give emotionally when she leaves the stage. "Show business can be a drug, a lover, and a whole lot of things," admits Warfield. "It fulfills that need. I don't need to inflict that on other people."

A career in comedy seemed like a foreign idea. There were no relatable role models. She was from a different mold than Moms or LaWanda Page. How do you become a working stand-up? When she met Elayne Boosler, it became clear. Warfield said the way was paved for her and others thanks to trailblazers such as Elayne, along with Judy Tenuta, Sandra Bernhard, Diane Nichols, Shirley Hemphill, and Shelly Pryor. Outside of Phyllis Diller, these women knew of no other stage comediennes, and it wasn't like they were having tea with Phyllis daily, so they made their own rules. In the case of Marsha Warfield, those rules worked.

By the time she made her arrival on *Night Court,* she was seasoned and had a reputation for reliability.

She had no acting experience, but her deadpan, straight delivery to bailiff counterpart Richard Moll was as good as team comedy gets and nobody in television gave a better cynical look. The Chicago native embodied Roz to critical and fan approval and had viewers in stitches from 1986 to 1992.

Marsha pulled double duty in 1990. She was so popular NBC slotted her with a self-titled daytime talk show where she and guests discussed hot topics of the day and got a load of laughs along the way. Her show was easy going and lasted for two seasons. Of course it didn't stop there. Following her run on *Night Court,* Warfield kept up her AFTRA status on the sitcom *Empty Nest,* playing Dr. Maxine Douglas from 1993 to 1995. She did major films (*D.C. Cab, Mask,* and *Caddyshack 2*), television guests spots (*Family Ties, Riptide,* and *Cheers*), and of course stand-up.

Then in 1995 tragedy struck. After her house was totaled in the Northridge earthquake, Marsha's mother and her sister died within three months of each other. Not long after her "lifestyle," as she described it, caught up with her and it took time to recover. By the time she was sober, a lot of time had passed in show-biz terms and newer faces had stepped in to fill the void. She returned to the stage and eventually moved to Las Vegas. From there she kept her presence known via social commentary on sites and remained a living inspiration to a whole generation of comediennes who followed in her footsteps.

"Marsha Warfield—the first black woman I ever seen do stand-up, and I still remember those jokes to this day and I was a kid. So, yeah, she was the first. She opened it up for me. So, yeah, I gotta give big ups to Marsha." —Nikki Carr

"She's one of the reasons I do stand-up comedy. Marsha Warfield is the first black female whose act I actually watched on national TV. I still remember some of her bits to this day."
—Alycia Cooper

"Very underestimated in her abilities. She started the phenomenon. She has a coolness; female Miles Davis, just smooth." —Thea Vidale

"That's my nigga." —Kym Whitley

"Oh my God, I just love Marsha. Now we're Facebook friends."
—Adele Givens

CHAPTER 13

Who Let the Girls Out?

"I was coming home from kindergarten—well, they told me it was kindergarten. I found out later I had been working in a factory for ten years. It's good for a kid to know how to make gloves."
—**Ellen DeGeneres**

The herstory of female comedy is filled with firsts. This comedienne was the first to do this. That comedienne was the first to do that. Firsts, firsts, firsts. So in all these groundbreaking incidences, invariably the name Ellen DeGeneres must come up. She's practically the queen of firsts. She was the first comedienne to be invited to sit down on the couch and talk to Johnny Carson immediately following her *Tonight Show* debut performance. She was the first comedienne to come out of the closet on a daytime talk show (*Oprah*). She was also the first leading character to have her supposed heterosexual character come out of the closet on a prime-time television sitcom. She was also the first comedienne to win a Saturn Award for her voice-over work as Dory in Pixar's *Finding Nemo*. And I'm sure before all is said and done, she will add even more firsts to her long list of esteemed credits. Oh, by the way—I hear she's a first-class individual as well.

ELLEN DEGENERES

The Louisiana native came from a sales background. Her father, Elliot, was an insurance agent. Her stepfather, Roy, was a salesman, and her brother, Vance, became a producer—and they're the biggest salesmen of all. Since the number-one rule of sales is to sell yourself, not the product, Ellen, by accident or design, has always been a salesperson herself. After leaving the University of New Orleans after one semester, she sold clothes at a retail department store and drank more liquor than a bartender.

In 1981, she sold Clyde's Comedy Club in New Orleans on the idea that she was the best person to be house MC, and in '82, Showtime was sold on that fact that she was the "funniest person in America." Carson got sold on her in 1986 (after twenty-four years of never having a female invited to the coveted couch), and Hollywood made its buy soon after.

From the late '80s to the mid-'90s, Ellen stayed busy doing television (*Open House*), films (*The Coneheads*), and comedy guest appearances. She got her first sitcom in 1994, originally called *These Friends of Mine* and later renamed *Ellen*. The show lasted until 1998, when ratings dropped after the coming-out episode, which was the peak during its run. During this period, DeGeneres was so popular Disney had her in a series of films at their Epcot Center focusing on energy conservation. *Ellen's Energy Adventure* was a huge attraction, as the comedienne dreamed she was playing the knowledge game *Jeopardy!* with Jamie Lee Curtis and Albert Einstein. Also around this time, DeGeneres had a much publicized relationship with actress Anne Heche that lasted four years.

Ellen's second sitcom on CBS didn't fare as well as the first. *The Ellen Show* debuted in 2001 and was canceled due to poor ratings in 2002. Seems without the controversy, the story of a lesbian leaving the rat race of the city to return to the slower existence of her small town hometown didn't strike a nerve with the public. Part of the problem might've been her reuniting with her former prom date, who thought they could pick up where they left off. Not even Ellen could sell that bill of goods to the public. So off went the show and off went Ellen back on the road to perform.

In 2003, Ellen returned to television as a daytime talk-show host. It was the year many took a stab at the format, but Ellen's show was special. She won four Emmys her first season. Audience giveaways and generous gifts to deserving schools and organizations helped push up the ratings.

"She is such a giving person; damn near Oprah. Oprah Jr. Damn, giving away stuff and making me cry when I watch her. That's some bullshit. I love it." —Adele Givens

Ellen danced on every show and sang with her audience off-camera. The national prejudice that plagued most gay celebrities seemed to have no effect on DeGeneres. She was the Teflon talker. She attracted high-profile guests even when she was hospitalized for a torn back ligament. Interviewees sat next to her hospital bed and chatted away.

In 2004, she gave them something else to talk about, when she began a relationship with Portia de Rossi, and they were engaged in May 2008 and married in California in August the same year. Their marriage was legally endangered when the state overturned same-sex marriages, but because they had their ceremony prior to November 4, the state Supreme Court validated the union.

Ellen sold herself to the public pretty much every time she put out the "for sale" sign. In 2001, she was selected to host the Emmy Awards after the 9/11 tragedy and opened by saying, "What would bug the Taliban more than seeing a gay woman in a suit surrounded by Jews?" In 2005, she hosted the prime-time Emmys three weeks after Hurricane Katrina, and the Academy Awards in 2007. It made her the first openly gay or lesbian person to have hosted the event. Her helming of the storied ceremony was so well received that morning talk-show mainstay Regis Philbin said, "The only complaint was there's not enough Ellen." She was nominated for an Emmy Award for her hosting duties on the Academy Awards broadcast.

Likeability was her stock in trade. Even when she crossed the picket line during the 2007 writers strike to uphold her contract and secure her ratings, she was still supported by AFTRA, though condemned by the WGA. She's written three books, received countless awards, founded her own record label (eleveneleven), judged on *American Idol,* was named Special Envoy for Global AIDS Awareness in 2011 by Secretary of State Hillary Clinton, and was the first open lesbian to be the face of Cover Girl cosmetics. Let's face it—we were all sold on Ellen.

Ellen opened the door to frank, honest talk regarding one's sexual preference. For ages homosexuals had guarded their lifestyle; otherwise, they'd be without the career that supported that lifestyle in fine fashion. Putting a recognizable face on any problem always brought greater awareness. So Ellen's honesty wasn't to alert people to the fact that there are gays in show business. It seemed more to say "gays you like." It was a cultural milestone, a tipping point and call for acceptance. It was a time of being yourself. Another who followed suit did so on her own talk show when she declared in 2002: "I'm a dyke."

ROSIE O'DONNELL

The Queen of Nice got her nickname for her lighthearted style. Surprising considering how many things had been taken from her. Cancer took her mother when Rosie was a preteen. When her liberal views as moderator on *The View* regarding the Iraq War conflicted with those of ABC, the network took her job. And definitely whenever she felt one of her causes was not being taken seriously, Rosie O'Donnell took herself on temper bouts.

The outgoing New Yorker was always into something. In high school she was voted homecoming queen, prom queen, class president, and class clown. She lost her comedy virginity playing Gilda Radner's Roseanne Rosannadanna in a high school skit. Once she graduated from there and dropped out of college, she hit the stand-up circuit. O'Donnell moved up quick in the comedy game. She won the talent show *Star Search* when she was twenty years old. The way it happened surprised even the overachiever. This is what she told talk-show host Larry King:

"I was twenty years old, and I was at a comedy club in Long Island. This woman came over to me and she said, 'I think you're funny. Can you give me your number? My dad is Ed McMahon.' I was like, yeah, right. I gave her my father's phone number. I was living at home, I'm like, whatever. And about three days later, the talent booker from *Star Search* called and said, 'We're going to fly you out to LA. . . . I won, like, five weeks in a row. And it gave me national exposure."

The aforementioned exposure was parleyed into the role as a neighbor on NBC's *Gimme a Break* starring Nell Carter. Two seasons later, she was hosting VH1's *Stand-Up Spotlight,* a show out to discover the next comedy star. In 1992, Rosie officially made the transition from TV to film after the FOX sitcom *Stand by Your Man* was canceled. She played Madonna's friend and scrappy baseball player in *A League of Their Own.* Others followed: *Sleepless in Seattle, The Flintstones, Exit to Eden,* and the voice of a female gorilla in Walt Disney's *Tarzan.*

O'Donnell returned to television in '96 with *The Rosie O'Donnell Show.* It was a daytime talk show that allowed her to be playful with her audience, as well as promote her various causes. Her love of Broadway plays was evident as O'Donnell welcomed cast members to guests on her show and by encouraging the audience to pluck down the bucks to see them, even when there were conflicts of principles. For instance, O'Donnell was for gun control, and when the cast from *Annie Get Your Gun* appeared on the show, she wanted them to change some of their rootin'-tootin' lyrics. Instead they sang another song. She lost her K-Mart contract for her anti-gun stance and strained her relationship with actor Tom Selleck when she confronted him about his support of the

NRA on her program. In 2002, the shop got closed.

It didn't help that her much heralded magazine, *Rosie,* was discontinued after two years following disputes with the publishers over its vision. They each sued each other for breach of contract, and a high-profile court case ensued. The outcome was a judge dismissing the case, in essence finding both sides had done wrong. (O'Donnell had been accused of verbally threatening a witness.) In 2002, she wrote a *New York Times* bestselling book, *Find Me,* a quasi-memoir. In 2003, she partnered to launch R Family Vacations, which offered vacation packages to gay and lesbian couples, their kids, friends, and parents. In 2004, she married her partner, Kelli Carpenter, and was a staunch advocate of same-sex marriage. The couple has three adopted children and a fourth conceived by artificial insemination to Kelli.

Rosie reemerged on television in 2006 on ABCs *The View.* It was to be a ride nobody would soon forget. Out the box, co-host Star Jones quit as O'Donnell came aboard. Some felt it might be their opposing views, where others felt it was because Rosie had stated Jones's rapid weight loss had to have been due to surgery and not diet and exercise, as Jones had alleged. Jones later admitted O'Donnell was right. She criticized the Catholic Church and its practice of relocating priests caught molesting young boys. For this she was called anti-Catholic, even though she herself was raised Catholic. She offended the Chinese community when she imitated a Chinese newscaster in a stereotypical fashion. Her subsequent apology was less than convincing. O'Donnell had a volatile feud with billionaire real estate mogul Donald Trump. It got so heated, he threatened to sue her and take away her life partner, Kelli. It stemmed from her criticism of his handling of the Miss America Beauty Pageant (which he owned). She was accused of calling US troops terrorists, which led to a dispute with conservative co-host Elisabeth Hasselbeck and O'Donnell's leaving the show.

Following her abdication as moderator for *The View,* Rosie started a blog. She won the 2007 Bloggers Choice Award. In

2009, she premiered a two-hour radio show on Sirius-XM. In 2011, Rosie debuted her new show, *The Rosie Show,* for OWN: Oprah Winfrey Network, and she continued to concentrate her efforts for gay and lesbian causes.

The battle for equality for all groups is a continuous one. From the time mankind began, even the smallest differences mattered, causing separation and distrust. Earthly habitation is brief and tenuous. So to spend non-refundable moments in the pursuit of the right to exist minus interference from opposing forces is an expenditure of time those forces obviously feel they can sacrifice. Non-idiots like to enjoy their lives. To fathom prejudice in any form is to condone the passing down of ignorance and bigotry. However, our history records organizations that protect rights and champion the causes of those receiving less-than-equal treatment. Like many comediennes within these pages, the multitalented Judy Gold devotes her precious moments to them.

JUDY GOLD

Dares are the way many careers in comedy get started. It's a testament to the individual who actually takes the dare and carries it through. It also speaks volumes when that same person pursues the dare to the point of a vocation. When it becomes a profession, it wasn't a dare. It was destiny. Judy Gold met hers at Rutgers University. She honed her act and got noticed. It didn't hurt that Judy stood 6' 3"—making getting noticed the norm. It got her on the ABC sitcom *All American Girl* starring Margaret Cho. It also got her on HBO as an on-the-spot interviewer asking people at the movie theater funny questions in segments called "At the Multiplex." That attention eventually landed her a gig writing and producing on *The Rosie O'Donnell Show,* where Gold won two daytime Emmys.

Not bad for a mother of two sons who has sustained a long-term relationship with her life partner. In 2006, Gold took her role as a mother and came up with her one-woman show, *25*

Questions for a Jewish Mother, with her writing partner, Kate Moira Ryan. It's based on her life with her mother, her life as a mother, and interviews with fifty Jewish mothers. In 2011, she was Off-Broadway with her production, called *Judy Gold: My Life as a Sitcom,* which received great reviews. Gold had struck again. The dare was well worth it and comedy was well served.

MO GAFFNEY

As previously stated, many comediennes lent their talents to a greater understanding of the gay and lesbian communities. In 2011, comedienne/playwright Mo Gaffney was one of the contributing writers on the Off-Broadway production of *Standing on Ceremony: The Gay Marriage Plays.* She's also officiated gay marriages after getting her certificate to oversee ceremonies. Gaffney gained prominence in the early '90s when she co-wrote the Off-Broadway show *The Kathy & Mo Show* along with friend Kathy Najimy. It won an Obie for Mo. That was 1991. In 1995, they repeated the task and received another Obie. She went on to host two of her own talk shows: *Women Aloud!* was on Comedy Central and *The Mo Show* aired on Fox.

CHAPTER 14

Let the Pillow Fights Begin

"Why do people say 'grow some balls'? Balls are weak and sensitive. If you wanna be tough, grow a vagina. Those things can take a pounding." —**Betty White**

The new millennium saw bold, new programming for sitcoms—groups of four women. It had to be funny, right? This trend was evident in *The Golden Girls, Designing Women, Sex and the City, Living Single,* and *Girlfriends*. They were all there to prove women could be friends and unite in their mutual distrust of men. Considering *Sex in the City* was created and written by a gay male, this was relationship storytelling once removed.

There is no monolith and each show took its own direction. HBO gave *Sex in the City* plenty of leeway. Sarah Jessica Parker, Kim Cattrall, Cynthia Nixon, and Kristin Davis had the room to shock. The double entendres and outright single entendres gave the comedy freedom to breathe. *The Golden Girls* had older women being as naughty as they pleased because, of course, they were older. *Living Single* had roommates and buddies (Kim Fields, Kim Coles, Queen Latifah, and Erika Alexander) who stopped by all the time. *Designing Women* had four Southern belles (Dixie Carter, Delta Burke, Annie Potts, and Jean Smart) and their on-again/ off-again love entanglements. Whereas *Girlfriends* (Tracee Ellis Ross, Golden Brooks, Persia White, and Jill Marie Jones) sometimes acted like they were anything but.

Most of these starred actresses that could do comedy. However, when it came to *The Golden Girls,* they had a cast that possessed comedy gems. Bea Arthur had already had her own show with *Maude.* Estelle Getty had originally made a name for herself in the Yiddish theater and as a comedienne in the Catskills borscht belt resorts. Rue McClanahan had done Broadway, soap operas, and *Maude,* but it was Betty White who rose so much she gave the phoenix exhaustion.

BETTY WHITE

Born on January 17, 1922, in Oak Park, Illinois, Betty Marion White was the daughter of a homemaker and a traveling salesman/electrical engineer. The family moved to California, where Betty went to school in Beverly Hills at Horace Mann School. That's where she discovered she had a knack for entertainment. She'd written a graduation play and played the lead.

Once she graduated high school, White went right into television. The year was 1939, and she found work on an experimental channel in Los Angeles singing songs along with another classmate. She modeled and acted in theater, and when World War II broke out, Betty joined the American Women's Voluntary Services. In 1945, she married US Army Air Corps pilot Dick Barker. That same year, she did radio programs, such as *Blondie,* and she soon had her own, *The Betty White Show.* The marriage to Barker dissolved, and in '47 she married Hollywood agent Lane Allen. That one didn't take either, ending in 1949. In 1952, she created the show *Life with Elizabeth*. It was syndicated and made Betty White one of the few women in television to have creative control on both sides of the camera. In 1954, she had her own talk show called—what else?—*The Betty White Show*. The remainder of the '50s saw White doing sitcoms and dog food commercials.

In the '60s, she was Queen of the Rose Parade and the First Lady of Game Shows (*Match Game, What's My Line?, To Tell the Truth,* and *Password*). *Password* was significant because White found her third, and last, husband in the form of the show's host Allen Ludden. She was the ideal American female, perfect down to the dimples. By the time the '70s rolled around, the idea of hiring a Betty White type to play a character on *The Mary Tyler Moore Show* was vetoed by Moore in favor of Betty White herself. White not only got the part, she got the joke and made sex-crazy homemaker Sue Ann Nevins a back-to-back Emmy winner.

White got a spin-off after *MTM* went off the air in '77. Believe it or not, it was called *The Betty White Show*. It lasted a season. After that, she jumped around doing guest-starring roles on sitcoms and miniseries. In 1981, Ludden died of bladder failure. She never remarried. From 1983 to 1985, White had a recurring role in *Mama's Family*. Once her run on that sitcom ended, Betty White became Rose Nylund on the top-rated hit *The Golden Girls*. She was told to play the character as terminally naïve, and that she did, to the tune of an Emmy win for Best Actress and a nomination for every year of the show's seven-season run. She got a spin-off, which oddly enough wasn't called *The Betty White Show*, but instead *The Golden Palace*. It lasted one season, and White was back on the guest-starring trail, picking up Emmy nominations and wins along the way.

It seemed the older Betty White got, the more she was in demand. After the year 2000, and while in her '80s, White had a role in the soap opera *The Bold and the Beautiful*. She had a recurring role on ABC's *Boston Legal*. She's done skits on late-night shows and been honored at award shows. White appeared in several motion pictures and some of the most talked about commercials of the decade. Then she decided to do another sitcom, this time playing a housekeeper on TV Land's *Hot in Cleveland*. She appeared in promotional videos for tourism, music videos for British singers, and is an advocate for animal rights and welfare.

Over the course of her long career, Betty White has won six Emmys and received twenty such nominations. She was the first woman to win for Best Game Show Hosting (for the short-lived *Just Men*). She got a prime-time Emmy Award in 2010 when she hosted *Saturday Night Live* and had the distinction of being the oldest person to ever do it. As a matter of fact, White was just as active, if not more so, in her later years than most performers are during their entire run. Point blank, Betty White's the hardest-working woman in show business and the only entertainer you can compare Betty White to is Betty White.

CHAPTER 15
Royalty Rules

"People drink and do drugs to go where I live." —**Monique Marvez**

Once upon a time, there was comedy royalty. Not Queen Moms, King Richard, Sir Redd, or Lady LaWanda. There was no Duke of Gregory, Count of Cosby, or Duchess of Goldberg. These new blue bloods were appointed; their lineage determined by a legislature of one. This royal line descended from the Kingdom of Latham. They were rated R by the citizenry. It was the year of our Lord 2001.

After scoring big with the original *Kings of Comedy* tour and concert film, comedy impresario Walter Latham naturally had to have a female version. Enter Mo'Nique, Sommore, Miss Laura Hayes, and Adele Givens. Each lady had her own following, but the combination fused the audiences into a crowd, culminating in a filming at the Orpheum Theatre in Memphis, Tennessee.

The formula was simple and played on each one's strengths. Miss Laura Hayes, a consummate storyteller, was the show's MC. She'd loosen the crowd up with tales about something they could all relate to—family. She'd introduce Adele Givens, who cracked them up with bits about her ninety-two-year-old grandmother, how you should watch what you name a baby, accepting the flaws you're stuck with, and how crazy the world has become. Sommore released the floodgates on kids, men, marriage, and motherhood (why moms give their eight-year-old daughters a Hula-Hoop). Lastly, Mo'Nique would come on and have a big girl-fest. Love your big self and feel free to hate the skinny heifers was the battle cry. The royals had honored the peasants with their presence, and Walter Latham had another hit.

MISS LAURA HAYES

She's describes herself as the "hip-hop baby boomer, part old-school/part new day. Oakland native Laura Hayes was best known to cable television watchers as the Cedric-obsessed, D'Militant-rejecting Miss Laura, who had all the right ingredients on BET's *Comic View*. Being featured daily gave her untold exposure and not only showed off her comedic skills, but her writing and biting wit as well. It was a departure from her former profession as a booster of fine women's and men's garments. Comedy provided Hayes with recurring roles (*Martin*), feature film roles (*I Got the Hook Up*), and an all-expenses-paid journey to the Kingdom of Latham. However, after a bad experience, this queen left the kingdom and returned from whence she came—to the Land of Acting.

"I retired in 2002 after the *Queens of Comedy* tour. I had a promoter tell me he was not going to pay me my $5,000. I became so angry I had a minor stroke, and two days later after I got out of the hospital, I retired from stand-up comedy because of that bad side of it. I was always trying to get my money. I got so tired of being the only bitch on the show, and you don't pay me or you lie to me or you trick me because you think I can't do shit about it. And after that happened, I knew because of the business side, I had to let it go."

ADELE GIVENS

A dele Givens got to the Kingdom of Latham via the Chicago comedy scene. Before ascending to the royal court, Adele proved her worth by winning the Crown Royal Comedy Contest in 1989 and causing a near sonic boom when she said on HBO's *Def Comedy Jam* that her sucking an overweight patron's penis with her big lips would be like a whale sucking a Tic Tac. That defining moment for feminine comedy catapulted Givens to the ranks of legendary, and she soon found herself co-hosting *Def Jam* (with Joe Torry and Ricky Harris) in 1995. Givens also made appearances on *Martin, Moesha, Tracey Takes On . . . ,* and the major motion picture *The Players Club*. She was known as such a fucking lady. She told us why:

"Back in the day when I first started, I noticed girls tend to be a little more icy towards you when you come onstage dressed up or made up or whatever, and that's how I felt more comfortable. I knew I was entertaining a group of people. So I didn't want to come there looking like, you know, shit— Miss Celie. That's where the term 'I'm such a fucking lady' originated. I was like I'm gonna be a fucking lady You're gonna let me do what I want to do. I'm not going to conform to the lady you perceive. Your ass is going to enjoy me as the fucking lady I am."

SOMMORE

A fter leaving Trenton, New Jersey, and heading for Southern California, Lori Ann Rambough, aka Sommore, started racking up wins. She won the Birdland Comedy Competition in Long Beach. She won the hosting spot on BET's *Comic View,* and she won the title of Queen of Comedy when she shared the royal stage with three other colleagues. Her style was smooth and accessible, raw yet endearing. Sommore looked and talked like a woman, but a woman other women liked, a rare combination for a comedienne. Usually if the men like a comedienne, the women don't. They view her as a threat.

"There's a lot to deal with being funny and an attractive female, but Sommore embraces it. She's going to come out with her cleavage, and I'm sure that was not easy in the beginning, but she's established a reputation for herself that she's going to bring it." —Iva Lashawn

Sommore was hot onstage, but offstage drama lurked. In February 2000, she was indicted for alleged narcotics trafficking. The *Washington Post* had reported that she was part of a drug ring and had been mailing packages of cocaine from Los Angeles to Washington in 1988. This began a year-long trial in Washington, D.C. She pleaded innocent, and on February 2, 2001, Sommore was found not guilty on all seven counts of drug conspiracy charges by a federal court judge. Fortunately the ordeal ended in time for the queen to resume her duties onstage and reap the benefits of the enormously successful tour.

After the *Queens of Comedy* was a memory, Sommore remained a top draw on the comedy circuit. She shied away from working with other females, preferring the perception that she's a comedian, funny without respect to gender. Like many, she bristled at the label. Forget the novelty—I'm funny. She proved this fact over and over on television (*Def Jam,* BET's *Live from L A,* and *Showtime at the Apollo*) film (*Friday After Next, Soul Plane,* and *Dirty Laundry*) and of course stages all over the world.

MO'NIQUE

The fourth child of a drug counselor father and engineer mother, queen Mo'Nique Angela Imes became an example of perseverance, strength, and the ability to excel. Once her brother, Steve, directed her to her destiny by daring Mo'Nique to get onstage at an open mike comedy night, there was no looking back. Mo'Nique put a spin on her name and a twist on being a big female comedian. Pride in her size was her mantra, and she put out product and a message to have other plus-size women join her crusade. After cutting her teeth in a Baltimore comedy spot she ran, Mo'Nique starred in a movie *Phat Girlz*. She put out a cookbook, entitled *Skinny Cooks Can't Be Trusted*. She parodied a Beyoncé's dance number "Crazy in Love" with other large females at the 2004 BET Awards, and she made big women proud of themselves in the process. Be who you are and love yourself was the theme, and it was long overdue.

Many were taken by surprise by her seemingly rapid ascension. Having already taped *Def Comedy Jam,* her second appearance got an unexpected two-fold jolt. The show's producers felt her choice of material did not serve her well and decided not to air it. That same night, she was plucked up by *Moesha* co-creator Ralph Farquhar for the role of Nikki Parker, Countess Vaughn's mother, on *Moesha* and the spin-off, *The Parkers*. That series made her a household name and lowered the drawbridge to the *Queens of Comedy* tour and concert film, radio (*Mo'Nique in the Afternoon*), more television (*Showtime at the Apollo, Flavor of Love Girls: Charm School,* and *The Mo'Nique Show*), a documentary (*I Could've Been Your Cellmate*), more films (*3 Strikes, Domino, Soul Plane,* and *Welcome Home, Roscoe Jenkins*), and a gang of awards, including the SAG, Golden Globe, BAFTA, and the coveted Academy Award for her searing performance as an abusive mother in the highly acclaimed motion picture *Precious.*

The *Queens of Comedy* set the stage for female empowerment in the taken-for-granted art form. There was still pay disparity and segregation in respect to bookings, but women were being sought out more, and the template was in place to reproduce its success. The wait wasn't long.

Beyond the Kingdom of Latham lay the Diva Castle. There all the Latin divas of comedy made their home. The land was inhabited by haters and doubters of the quartet, but none believed in them more than themselves and the fans who went to witness the awesome spectacle of Marilyn Martinez, Sara Contreras, Monique Marvez, and Sandra Valls stripping the paint off the walls.

The impresario behind this curtain was string puller/comedian Alex Reymundo. He was executive producer, along with Sarah Wasserman, Bob Abramoff, Scott Montoya, and Neal Marshall. As with the queens, the divas had the lead-in of a Latin kings phenomenon. So the template was in place. All Reymundo had to do was select the right blend of talent, and he'd be assured another hit. Then again he didn't want the divas looking exactly like the queens; that's why when a man (in this case, Reymundo) stepped onstage as host of the taping at the California Theatre in San Bernardino in November 2006, it was a move approved by his extremely supportive male boss.

Reymundo's picks featured a diverse crew of female talent. There was Sandra Valls, the Mexican lesbian who grew up in Texas. From Jersey, he got Sara Contreras, a Puerto Rican single mom sacrificing all by living in an upper-class Jewish neighborhood. Marilyn Martinez was a veteran and refrained from being nasty her whole set. She stopped talking after each sentence. It was capped off by Monique Marvez, a Cuban from Miami, who never met a truth she didn't like to talk about.

SANDRA VALLS

This multitalented diva breaks all the stereotypes of divadom. For one, she's a stand-up comedian. Two, a woman of Hispanic descent. Three, Sandra Valls is a Latina *lesbian* comedienne. The former singer who performed at her own prom stretched out her tentacles and went into producing after landing a job on a hit show on Latin cable television network Mun2. She produced *Off the Roof* and served as its writer and on-camera reporter. It covered entertainment and special human interests stories on Latinos. Sandra's been featured on *Comic View, The Latino Laugh Festival, HBO Latino,* and *Que Locos!*

SARA CONTRERAS

This diva has smarts. She gained recognition after becoming a semifinalist at the Funniest Teacher contest at Stand-Up NY in 1995. In 1997, she became a pioneer. Sara was the first East Coast Latina to achieve a spot at the Latino Laugh Festival in San Antonio. She was representing New York. She continued her trailblazing spirit as a founding member of the comedy troupe Sisters Doing Comedy. Her television credits include Comedy Central's *Comic Groove,* ABC's *The View,* Metro Channel's *New Joke City,* A&E's *American Comedy: What's So Funny?,* SITV's *Funny Is Funny* and *The Show,* and TC Network's *Que Loco.* Besides keeping it moving in her career, Contreras liked to keep it moving on-stage.

"I see people who have been doing comedy a long time doing the same material over and over again, and they're bringing it and they're doing well. It's working for them. I can't do that. I get bored. But then I look back on a DVD and go, damn, that's a good joke. Why did I stop doing it?"

MONIQUE MARVEZ

With an hourglass shape and a razor-sharp wit, Monique Marvez makes stand-up look easy. She effortlessly slays comedy audiences seeking to derive their laughs from the real. When you see Monique, you know why she's so unique. Her persona is like a big sister or trusted neighbor. You know she'll tell you what's on her mind whether you want to hear it or not. You also know she speaks from wisdom, so it's best you listen up.

Her career has taken her all over the map of mediums. She's been featured in the Montreal Comedy Festival, as a guest on *Montel Williams,* and was the hostess of *Penthouse* magazine's twenty-fifth-anniversary special. She's also appeared on Comedy Central's *Comics on Delivery.* But it was her one-woman show, *Loca Motive,* that got the attention of Barry Diller's Silver King Broadcasting. In no time, the Sage with Rage was hosting her own show, *Monique Over Miami,* and *Lady Zings the Blues,* as well as *Monique and the Man,* where she had the number-one show in her demographic.

MARILYN MARTINEZ

The grand diva of all these ladies was Marilyn Martinez. At the time of her untimely passing, Marilyn was a thirty-year vet. She was truly uncompromising in what formulated in her nimble brain and came out of her pouty lips. Marilyn was a round woman with an even rounder face and a heart that had to have been perfectly shaped. Despite her "in charge" demeanor onstage, Martinez was the epitome of a good, caring friend offstage. Marilyn inhabited a world of two kinds of people: those who knew her and were her friends and those who hadn't met her yet, but once they did would be her friends.

Marilyn was a regular at the world-famous Comedy Store in Hollywood and one of club owner Mitzi Shore's favorites. She toured with Paul Rodriguez (nearly one hundred shows). Pauly Shore featured her in his 2003 film, *Pauly Shore Is Dead.* She also hit the road with Joe Rogan and Paul Mooney. Marilyn appeared on Showtime's *Latino Laugh Festival, Funny Is Funny,* and *Que Loco's* and ABC's *The Damon Wayan's Show.* She was a regular on SiTV's reality show *Urban Jungle,* where she played Madrina (the godmother) to a house full of spoiled kids. Films include *Choose Life* (landlord), *You'll Never Work in This Town Again* (maid), *For Da Love of Money* (receptionist), *El Matador* (love interest), *The Cheapest Movie Ever Made* (land lady), and *Camera Obscura.*

Marilyn Martinez was dear to many people. Her goal was to make others feel better. Unfortunately for those very same people, Marilyn would not be around as long as they wanted. She was diagnosed with colon cancer. Thus began nine anguish-filled months from her husband, David, loyal friends, family, and fans. The one most at peace throughout it all was

Martinez, who passed away quietly on November 3, 2007, surrounded by loved ones. That's all she ever had anyway.

***

Turned out Marilyn was more than a hilarious comedienne. She was the link to the first recognized Latina comedy troupe, the Hot and Spicy Mamitas. That stand-up comedy show was born in 1994 out of a need for Latina comedians to be seen. The show was created by Lydia Nicole, Sully Diaz, and Ludo Vika, who were performing at the Comedy Store in Hollywood but were having a difficult time getting booked regularly at other venues because there was no club outside of the Comedy Store who would put more than two females, let alone Latinas, on a nightly bill together.

Well, it just so happened that Lydia Nicole had just finished co-producing another comedy show called *Funny Ladies of Color* that ran out of the Comedy Store, featuring Lotus Wienstock, Sherri Shepherd, Cha Cha Sandoval, Jackie Guerra, Christy Medrano, Carlease Burke, Alexis Rhee, Loretta Colla, Kathy Westfield, Cynthia Levin, Laurie Kay, Dyana Ortelli, and Sandy Brown. Within a month the Mamitas was born. Following the departure of Debi Gutierrez, the group featured Lydia Nicole, Sully Diaz, Ludo Vika, Marilyn Martinez, and Dyana Ortelli, giving it the representation of various Latino backgrounds, including a Puerto Rican, a Nuyorican, a Mexican, a New Mexican, and a Dominican.

Like most new things they faced opposition. The Improvisation's founder, Budd Friedman, famously stated, "I don't like them individually, and I definitely don't like them as a group." No matter.

They were at the Comedy Store and adored by the Latin and local press, who declared, "The Mamitas deliver a show with the heat of jalapenos." Each comedienne brought her own style to the mix. Sully Diaz, the virgin diva mother; Marilyn Martinez, the Rocky Mountain hellion; Lydia Nicole, the Harlem *princesa;* Dyana Ortelli, Mexican most wanted; and Ludo Vika, the Caribbean Queen. Together they burned up stages and left them in ashes.

It was a bombardment of females being irreverent, outspoken, and undeniably delicious. These women teamed up in June 1994 to bring forth a hilarious ninety-minute extravaganza. And they continued to perform and dazzle audiences for the next six years. They toured and gained notoriety with their self-titled debut CD on the Uproar label and set the stage for the queens and divas. All of these pioneering women ruled their kingdoms with unflinching hilarity and paved the way for future funny monarchs.

CHAPTER 16

Saturday Night's All Right

"I've seen too much money and too much stuff turn people into assholes." —**Nora Dunn**

aturday Night Live made a rebound in part due to its women. The venerable NBC mainstay had seemed to have overstayed its welcome a horde of times since its 1975 debut, but recent years had the most ardent fans laying out their clothes for the funeral. It wasn't nostalgic yearnings for the old days either. It was just plain unfunny. Then came the 2008 presidential campaign and the return of Tina Fey as Republican vice presidential nominee Sarah Palin and cast member Amy Poehler as Democratic presidential candidate Hillary Clinton. They sparred together with classic results. It's guaranteed to make the time capsule. Hilarious television. The ratings shot back up, coveted guest hosts wanted to host, and the writers got funnier . . . or fired. The beast was again loose.

The maiden crew had raised the bar—high. Gilda Radner,

Jane Curtin, and Laraine Newman became what every comedienne wanted to be at the time—employed.

GILDA RADNER

The character chameleon was born into privilege. Her Jewish parents had a fine home in Detroit and Gilda had a nanny she named Dibby. She grew up with a brother, Michael, and an eating disorder that had a doctor prescribe the ten-year-old Gilda Dexedrine diet pills. Her father, a hotel operator and Gilda's tour guide into the world of Broadway shows, developed a brain tumor and died two years later when Gilda was fourteen.

A camera first got its glimpse of Gilda as a professional when she became the weather girl for college radio station WCBN. In 1972, she left her senior year to follow her boyfriend to Toronto, Canada. Once there she joined the Second City comedy troupe. That group boasted the talents of Catherine O'Hara, Andrea Martin, and Robin Duke. From 1974 to 1975, Gilda was featured on the *National Lampoon Radio Hour,* along with John Belushi, Bill Murray, Brian Doyle-Murray, Richard Belzer, and Chevy Chase.

Gilda was the first performer cast for *Saturday Night Live.* From the show's inception until 1980, she created indelible characters such as Roseanne Roseannadanna, Baba Wawa, and Emily Litella. She'd nail celebrities like Lucille Ball, Olga Korbut, and Patti Smith in hilarious sketches. She dealt with her bulimia throughout her stay and had a relationship with fellow cast member Bill Murray that ended poorly. She hated to be recognized by fans in public, but hated it even more when she wasn't noticed. And for all her efforts, Gilda was awarded an Emmy in 1978.

In 1979, Gilda had a successful one-woman Broadway show, *Gilda Radner—Live from New York!* The following year, acclaimed director Mike Nichols shot the presentation for the theatrical release *Gilda Live!* and it bombed. The soundtrack album bombed too. Seems the only ray of sunshine from that 1980 experience was Gilda meeting future husband, G. E. Smith, a musician on the show. They were married that same year.

The union of Radner and Smith rapidly deteriorated. In stepped Gene Wilder while on the set of Sidney Poitier's *Hanky Panky,* and Gilda said it was "love at first sight." They made another film together in 1984 (*The Woman in Red*) and married that fall in the south of France. Their third movie together was 1986's *Haunted Honeymoon;* the same year, she was diagnosed with ovarian cancer. When she went into remission, Gilda wrote the book *It's Always Something,* and *Life* magazine did a cover story on her illness. Radner guest-starred on Showtime's *It's Garry Shandling Show* and was scheduled to host *Saturday Night Live* when the writers' strike curtailed that plan.

On May 17, 1989, Gilda went into Cedars-Sinai in Los Angeles, California, for a CAT scan. She flew into a panic, refusing to stay on the gurney, so she was given a sedative, lapsed into a coma, and died three days later on May 20. Gene Wilder was by her side at the end, but by his own account, regrettably did not say "good-bye" before she slipped out of consciousness for the last time. Her gravestone reads, "Gilda Radner-Wilder—Comedienne / Ballerina 1946–1989." She was forty-two years old.

"When I think of Gilda, I think of the wonderful character she created and I tend to get a little sad, but when I get sad like that I start thinking, well, at least I have her going, 'This is Babawawa.' That is like the ultimate thing to leave this earth and somebody can still remember you forty, fifty, sixty years. She did that." —Loni Love

JANE CURTIN

"The Queen of the Deadpan" was born in Cambridge, Massachusetts, on September 6, 1947. She was brought up Roman Catholic and her dad owned an insurance agency.

Hopefully he didn't anticipate her following him into the family business, because in 1968 she dropped out of college to pursue a future in comedy. She joined the comedy group the Proposition and stayed with them until 1972. It was in 1975 that Jane got her career changer by landing a spot as a "not ready for primetime" player on *Saturday Night Live*. It was a great gig for her creatively. Since she was a serious Catholic and married, a gig was all it was for Jane Curtin. The drugs, alcohol, and partying side were left to other cast members. Jane anchored "Weekend Update" from 1976 to 1977 and then co-anchored with Dan Ackroyd (1977–78) and Bill Murray (1978–1980). She also became known for her "Point-Counterpoint" sketches with Ackroyd and for playing mother Conehead.

Jane Curtin's post-*SNL* career trajectory was decidedly different from those of her original cohorts. Instead of popping up in film comedies, she remained on TV and gained a strong reputation.

From 1984 to 1989, Jane co-starred opposite Susan Saint James in the sitcom *Kate & Allie,* where she received Emmy Awards as Best Lead Actress on two occasions. She followed up that success with the part of Dr. Mary Albright on ABCs *3rd Rock from the Sun* from 1996 to 2001. *Crumbs* on the same network was her next outing, but it only lasted four months.

"People played off of her even in subsequent jobs. She still never was the person with the line that got the laugh. She was always the person that set up the laugh. When she worked on 3rd Rock *she was the one who set up the joke."* —Jedda Jones

Jane Curtin has narrated documentaries, guest-starred on sitcoms, competed on game shows (*Jeopardy!*), voiced several audiobooks, and generally had a full career as a comedienne.

LARAINE NEWMAN

Laraine Newman's journey to *Saturday Night Live* stardom took her across the country. Born in Los Angeles, California, on March 2, 1952, Laraine grew up with three other siblings, one being her twin. After graduating from Beverly Hills High School, she was one of the founding members of the Groundlings and *Saturday Night Live*. The latter ran from 1975 to 1980. During her tenure on the groundbreaking show, she played everything from Valley girls to a Conehead extraterrestrial.

Once *SNL* was a thing in Laraine's past, she set out to guest-star on every show casting humans. *Laverne & Shirley, St. Elsewhere, According to Jim, 3rd Rock from the Sun, Friends,* and *Curb Your Enthusiasm* have all had a Laraine Newman episode. She did voice work on *WALL-E, Cars, Up!, Finding Nemo,* and *SpongeBob SquarePants.* She's also worked as a writer, editor, and contributor for *The Huffington Post.*

✳✳✳

These three foremothers laid the foundation for the women that followed. Their spot-on impressions and characterizations influenced an entire generation of comediennes on the way to do it, if evidenced by those that followed. For when it comes to female talent, *SNL* knew how to treat the ladies. Let's take a look at the impressive roster: Ellen Cleghorne, Joan Cusack, Rachel Dratch, Christine Ebersole, Janeane Garofalo, Mary Gross, Victoria Jackson, Julia Louis-Dreyfus, Abby Elliot, Molly Shannon, Sarah Silverman, Maya Rudolph, Julia Sweeney, Nancy Walls, and the maverick Nora Dunn. Saturday night always looked like ladies night.

Over the years the show has taken its hits. Most of the time when it was maligned, it was due to lack-of-comedic content. Other times it was accusations of not enough racial diversity in the female category. In a city as culturally varied as New York (where the program is shot live) such claims seem to stick.

B-Phlat agrees with the racial aspect, with gender having

little bearing: "I only watched it to see Eddie's part. I just wasn't into that slapstick-type of comedy. I don't know. That's probably the prejudice in me. We all have our prejudices. *Saturday Night Live* had John Belushi and all them sliding around onstage acting stupid. My daddy would say, 'Turn that shit off.' We couldn't watch it if it didn't have any black people in there."

So for a number of races, lack of representation kept them from becoming loyal fans. Then there were times *SNL* became a lightning rod for controversy based on principle. In 1990, cast member Nora Dunn refused to appear on the show the night Andrew "Dice" Clay guest-hosted. Sinead O'Connor made a similar decision, but it was Dunn's MIA that struck a comedy cord.

NORA DUNN

N ora Dunn entered show business with an entertainment pedigree. Her father, John, was a musician/poet; her brother, Kevin, was an actor. Nora got on *SNL* the season Lorne Michaels returned after a disastrous previous season. The founder of the show got it back on its feet, keeping Dunn and few other cast members from the debacle that had been the 1985–'86 cast.
Nora Dunn recalls those days:

"When I first arrived there on the show, I was surprised not to see a lot of people I had worked with in San Francisco, such as Dana Carvey. They didn't go that way the second year when they got people on who were comedians and improvisers and had that history behind them. They tried something different, which clearly didn't work.

"The first night we were all going to be on audition. Dennis Miller and I went to dinner with Lorne Michaels and six or seven other people at the dinner table. I had never been to a restaurant like the restaurant he took us to. I wasn't hired yet to be on *Saturday Night Live*. I was worried about money. They kept us in a hotel. They didn't give us any per diem. So I'm like I'm going on week two here and I don't know what's going on.

"So we're coming out of the restaurant and Jack Nicholson and Anjelica Huston were sitting at a table. They asked us—they knew Lorne, of course—to sit down and have dinner and drinks with them. Well, I saw Jack Nicholson and, y'know—oh my God. He's the iconic figure of the '70s. He was *Five Easy Pieces, The Last Detail, One Flew Over the Cuckoo's Nest.* He was *Chinatown* and I was just awestruck. I couldn't sit down at the table. I just was like, what am I going to do?

"I'm a middle child, an invisible person. I didn't like people asking me questions or looking at me much. I just couldn't deal with it. So I thought I better go to the ladies room and collect myself, then I'll come back. But I went out the wrong door and it was raining out and I started getting wet. But I just stood there and I thought, 'I'm getting wet. They're going to ask me why am I all wet.' Then I got completely drenched. So I didn't go back into the restaurant. I just went out to the limo and waited.

"The limo driver was smoking pot. He offered me some, so I got kind of stoned. 'Now I'm really in another world,' I thought. 'I was waitressing last week; now I'm having after-dinner drinks with Jack Nicholson.' I smelled like a dog. But no one mentioned why I didn't come back to the table or that I was soaked and wet when everyone came back to the limo. It was Dennis Miller who later mentioned it to me, that I gave the impression that I didn't care at all about those big movie stars."

She was an integral part of the resurgence, playing a wide range of characters, from Pat Stevens, the model turned talk show host, to Loose Chang (the name says it all) to one half of the singing Sweeney Sisters (Jan Hooks being the other half). Once Dunn left the show after a five-season run, she made films and guest-starring appearances. However, it was the stand against the misogynistic Dice Clay that Dunn will be best remembered.

Nora tells exactly how it all happened.

You like political humor.

"I grew up in the '60s and so politics, a lot of the big improv groups, if you went to see them, they talked not so much about politics, but the politics of life. The Vietnam War was going when I was in high school. The civil rights movement was going on all through the '60s. So I grew up in that period of marches, of a lot of descent. That's just a natural thing for me because when I was in grade school and high school, I graduated high school in 1970, so all of that stuff happened. And so it was a part of my life. It wasn't something you had to dig deep for. A lot of the humor of the comedians of that day, Woody Allen and these kinds of people that came out of all that, it was woven right into their work. So for me that's where all that comes from. My family was political. My parents were involved in all these kind of movements. Everyone in those days had an opinion and took a side. The ten years of the '60s were all about really major, major shifts in the culture."

Andrew "Dice" Clay.

"The thing about Andrew 'Dice' Clay, how popular he became; forget the topic of his material, but he's not funny. Not funny and he represents a huge group of threatened men: homophobic, misogynistic. And why on earth did anybody think he should host *Saturday Night Live,* which is an honor, even though there's been how many? Hundreds and hundreds of shows and it's still an honor to host the show, and so when you choose a host, you're honoring him and you're honoring what he stands for and you're honoring his material. It wasn't just dumb, it wasn't just mean, it was dangerous. It was part of people who came to my neighborhood to beat up fags. All his stuff about women was beyond degrading and it wasn't funny.

"Like I said, I grew up in the '60s where everybody took a stand. In the '60s, I was in those marches. My parents made us march in some of those marches. I come from that, and people on the show . . . I was older. Even if you missed that by five years, you missed it. My allegiance is not to NBC and my allegiance is not to *Saturday Night Live.* That was my job, so you know I feel very strongly about it and I felt very emotional about it and I wish I hadn't been so emotional about it. But it was like I only had two more shows to do. I didn't want to write another sketch for as long as I lived, and had that not happened I fulfilled my contract. It was no disputes and I wasn't fired. A lot of people say I was dumped. That's nutso. I was not coming back after my five years. I didn't have any reason to."

What advice do you have for anybody following in your footsteps?

"I went back to *Saturday Night Live,* which was fun. I think the difference in the women now that are dominating the scene at *Saturday Night Live* is that they don't think about it, and that's great. The whole idea of forging a trail, if indeed I did, or anybody did, I don't consider myself as somebody who's forged a trail. I have to look at Lily Tomlin, Joan Rivers, people who really have these huge careers and made a big impact. The idea of forging a trail is so other people can use the trail. They don't necessarily have to know who came before them. I think that's the thing about any kind of movement, to make it a given."

What other things did you do after SNL?

"At the time, I wanted to do stuff that was a little more meaningful or serious. I was way too picky. I didn't understand just go out and take a job. I ended up on *Sisters,* which was a really good thing for me. So I did that series for three years, an NBC series and I was writing at that time. Eventually I wrote my one-woman show, got that up. I've done movies, television; I've had a very good career and a very good life along with it.

JULIA LOUIS-DREYFUS

Another cast member living a good life was Julia Louis-Dreyfus. For her it started out that way. Her dad was a billionaire heir to the family business, Louis Dreyfus Group, and her cousin was a former CEO of Adidas and owned his own soccer team (mom was a writer). She grew up in faraway lands such as Sri Lanka, Colombia, and Tunisia and left Northwestern University (where she met future husband Brad Hall) after three years of theater study.

Julia got her invitation to appear on *Saturday Night Live* after developing as an artist working improv at the Practical Theater Group and Second City. She was only twenty-one, the youngest female cast member in the show's history (along with Abby Elliot). Julia was at *SNL* from 1982 to 1985, working along with talents such as Eddie Murphy, Billy Crystal, and Martin Short and playing recurring characters:

- April May June, a televangelist
- Becky, El Dorko's (Gary Kroeger) date
- Consuela, Chi Chi's friend and co-host of "Let's Watch TV"
- Darla in *SNL*'s parody of *The Little Rascals*
- Weather Woman, a superhero who controls the weather
- Patti Lynn Hunnsucker, a teenage correspondent on "Weekend Update"

It's also where she met future benefactor, Larry David. After leaving *Saturday Night Live,* Julia had roles in Woody Allen's *Hannah and Her Sisters* and *National Lampoon's Christmas Vacation* with Chevy Chase. In 1987, she married Brad Hall and then it was back to television in the NBC sitcom *Day by Day.* It was canceled after thirty-three episodes..

The '90s came and so did *Seinfeld.* The co-creation of Jerry Seinfeld and Larry David was lightning in a bottle for nine record-breaking seasons. Julia beat out Rosie O'Donnell, Megan Mullally, and Patricia Heaton for the coveted part of Elaine Benes, an after-thought character ordered after NBC execs decided the pilot was too dudey. That whim creation won Julia an Emmy (seven nominations), a Golden Globe, and five SAG Awards. Elaine was one of the guys, but all girl. Her hair changed every season, but she never changed her wise-cracking, sex-happy ways. Elaine was a girl guys actually could hang out with . . . for a while anyway.

When *Seinfeld* left the air in 1998, Julia lent her voice to animated films and sitcoms and made guest appearances. On HBO's *Curb Your Enthusiasm,* she played herself, mocking the *Seinfeld* curse of not being able to be in a successful show after Jerry's. The real Julia broke that curse (for a while) in 2002 with *Watching Ellie* for NBC. That one lasted two seasons. Not enough time to fully topple the spell. In 2006, she found the potion at CBS. The show was called *The New Adventures of Old Christine.* It made it for five seasons, with Julia playing the elder of two women named Christine in her ex-husband's life. Thus old Christine (or ex-Christine). Either way, she won another Emmy, for Lead Actress this time (first season).

Julia was the first former female *SNL* cast member to return to host the show. She has done it a total of three times. Post-*Christine,* she also found a home at HBO in 2012 for her starring role as the vice president in *Veep.* So serious was Julia about the part, she contacted former vice president Al Gore for a consultation. Not bad for a rich kid.

Despite its imperfections, the *Saturday Night Live*'s output of talent can't be denied. And no comedienne has been more impressive than Tina Fey. By sheer accomplishments and accolades alone, she's in a class all by herself—female or male. An alumni of Chicago's Second City, the writer/actress/producer/author has managed, in a career spanning a mere seventeen years, to amass seven Emmys, four Screen Actor Guild Awards, three Golden Globes, and four Writer Guild of America Awards. Fey's film *Mean Girls* had a worldwide box office take of $129 million. *Baby's Mama* made $64 million, and *Mega Mind* pulled down $321 million worldwide. Ummmm . . .

TINA FEY

Elizabeth Stamatina Fey wasn't always the life of the award show circuit. Born in the small township of Upper Darby, Pennsylvania, "Tina" lived a comfortable youth with her older brother, Peter, and her Greek mother and German-Scottish father. Her comedy virginity was broken by old Marx Brothers movies and *Honeymooner* episodes. Her father forbade the viewing of *The Flintstones* since he deemed them a *Honeymooners* rip-off. However, she was allowed to watch *Second City TV* and adopt Catherine O'Hara as the woman she wanted to be one day.

Tina Fey wasn't going to let too many days pass before she shot for that goal. During middle school, she did a project on the subject of comedy. Then Tina went to work on learning her chosen craft by studying playwriting and acting in college, earning a degree in drama; next stop—Second City and total immersion in the religion of improvisation. The year was 1994 and her apprenticeship consisted of eight shows a week for two years. She took a stab at stand-up, but realized her strength lied in improvisation.

Besides being quick on her feet and having a nimble wit, Fey was also a writer with a wicked pen. In 1997, she got her *SNL* gig by submitting scripts, which got the attention of then-head writer Adam McKay, who suggested her for a paid writing slot. Initially her sketches had difficulty getting aired, but it wasn't long before she caught on, and when McKay stepped down, Fey was hired by show creator Lorne Michaels to take his place. Then she took personal improvement to the next level and lost thirty pounds to make her physical package more TV friendly after seeing herself on camera. Following that version of scaling back, she got approached to do a lot more sketches.

In 2000, she got the coveted co-anchor position on *SNL*'s "Weekend Update," along with Jimmy Fallon. This job was the launching pad to stardom for the likes of Chevy Chase, Dan Aykroyd, and Dennis Miller. Fey was now not only the first female head writer for the show, but according to alumni Miller—the funniest "anchor" to ever sit at the "Weekend Update" desk. When Fallon left the show in 2004, he was replaced by Amy Poehler, making it the first time two women shared the duties of presenting the mock news.

30 Rock had already been green-lit by NBC by the time Fey left *SNL* at the end of the 2006 season. It had actually been a rejected pilot idea she presented in 2002 to a cable affiliate of NBC. In 2003, she signed a renewal contract for *SNL,* which also allowed her to develop a sitcom. As soon as she left in 2006, *30 Rock* made its premiere in October of that year and ranked very poorly. Regardless, NBC stuck with it and the show became a critical darling, if not a ratings blockbuster. Fey and the show won so many awards that you forgot there were other nominees.

On top of all the industry recognition, Fey became a cultural phenomenon. Between September 2008 and March 2011, she impersonated Sarah Palin a half dozen times, with the September 13 maiden voyage holding the distinction of going viral to the tune of 5.7 million hits (a *SNL* record), and the October 18, 2008, sketch where Fey meets the real Sarah Palin being the highest rated episode since 1994. She's been ranked as hot and beautiful by *Maxim* and *People* magazines, respectively, and voted one of the fifty most powerful women by the *New York Post.* And did we forget to mention that in 2011 Tina Fey was *Forbes* magazine's highest paid TV actress.

✳✳✳

Well, not every comedienne is going to be a Tina Fey, but she's a yardstick; something to aspire to be, and she's just hitting her stride.

Another SNL comedienne running her own strong race had audiences asking who she was before they could pronounce her name.

KRISTEN WIIG

Thanks to a number of strong supporting and walk-on roles in films like *Knocked Up, Ghost Town,* and *Forgetting Sarah Marshall,* Wiig was already a stand-out, noticeable talent when she starred in the mega-hit she co-wrote with Annie Mumolo, 2011's *Bridesmaids.* The two former Groundling members struck gold at the box office with a $280 million worldwide gross. It co-starred Maya Rudolph, Rose Byrne, Ellie Kemper, Wendi-McClendon-Covey (*Reno 911!*) and the breakout star, Melissa McCarthy (*Mike & Molly*). The film made big money at the box office and allowed Wiig to follow the tradition of previously successful *SNL* cast members (and sometimes not so successful) to leave the show for a film career.

✳✳✳

So have we debunked the Jerry Lewis notion shared by many males, comedians and civilian alike, that women are not funny? You probably laughed a gang of times just reading about them and reliving many of the moments and memories you'd forgotten about. That's the beauty of comedy. Sometimes when the joke isn't even being told, the thought of it makes you smile. Thankfully women have made us all smile our entire lives, but what does the future hold?

CHAPTER 17
Straight, No Chaser

"Guys don't have to go onstage on their periods, having cramps after arguing with your man. I've been onstage having a miscarriage." **—Luenell**

The boom on both fronts had long since ended. Stars had been made, empires built. The onslaught of comedy wannabes had subsided and calm once again ruled the day. The amount of clubs, shows, audience, and revenue had declined considerably. Part of it was due to a recession that began in October 2008 and left in its crippling path closed businesses of all sorts, high unemployment, government bailouts to major corporations, ruined lives, and a climate of despair. You'd have thought people would need a good laugh more than ever. They did—just couldn't afford to pay for it.

Many comedians found themselves doing the unspeakable—taking day jobs.

"I actually quit for a year to go to naked pool parties. It seemed easier to get booked to get naked." —Henrietta

Then comedy began making a comeback, having a resurgence. As the economy and unemployment figures improved, so did the entertainment industry. Retirees and semi-retirees are returning to retest the waters. Kids had been birthed.

"You find a working ovary in here, you need to bronze that thing and put it up on the mantle. I'm done. I had two kids I finished raising. I don't even know what kind of grandma I'm going to be. I'm not going to knit them sweaters. I'm knitting a parachute for them when I throw them out the window."

—Sara Contreras

Marriages had been dissolved due to lack of common goals. Seemed not every comedienne was cut out to just be a housewife.

"I was actually a housewife. I would like to be a housewife again if I could still do stand-up." —Thea Vidale

So the atmosphere was ripe for disturbance, and the new millennium crop of comediennes is unabashedly in your face. They expect the freedom to say what the guys do, and more if they want. Led by the examples of Mae West, Joan Rivers, and the ilk, these new ladies are not only ready for prime time, they took over cable and the Internet while nobody was looking. With book deals, talk shows, production companies, and projects galore, comedy has not seen a stronger field of females since the expression "stand-up comic" was coined in 1966. Thanks needs to go to their foremothers, but they also have pioneering sisters in their midst.

KATHY GRIFFIN

Kathleen Mary Griffin pulled back a layer of the show-biz onion and exposed the fact that the stink can be nutritious too. Instead of lamenting and bucking the fact she'd only received moderate notoriety after years of steady work, she parlayed it into a multimillion-dollar self-deprecating joke on the industry. If they were going to make disposable stars, she'd be one of them, except one with talent, wit, and savvy who knew how to play it.

The Illinois-born baby boomer first got our attention on February 22, 1996, in the *Seinfeld* episode "The Doll." In it Griffin plays Sally Weaver, the former roommate of George Costanza's fiancée, Susan. After a comedy of errors, Sally blows Jerry's chance to appear on *The Charles Grodin Show* twice. This experience led to Griffin lambasting the real Seinfeld in her HBO special, to the delight of her victim. He not only wrote her a note saying how much he loved her skewering him and saying he was rude to her, he had her back on the show for another go at the character. This time they mocked Griffin's real-life diss on *Seinfeld* as Sally got her own cable special blasting Jerry fictionally.

Griffin played that David-vs.-Goliath act right to the bank. The D-list mentality was born and the show soon followed. Why try to give the perception you're a big shot when everybody knows you're not? She embraced her low rung on the ladder, and Bravo gave her the wood to build it. After starting with the Groundlings, doing the stand-up circuit, appearing in *Pulp Fiction* (don't blink), co-starring on Brooke Shields's *Suddenly Susan* and her own comedy specials and guest-starring spots, Kathy Griffin made her lack of celebrity the inside joke that everybody got.

"I think she's done some stuff that just makes me laugh, and then there's another part of me that's like, wow, if she can make it, how come I can't? I know that sounds terrible, but I feel very strongly about that." —Di Stanky

Griffin's show lasted five seasons (from 2005 to 2010) and placed Griffin on red carpets (as commentator), on Broadway, on the bestseller list for her books, and at award ceremonies as a winner of a GLAAD, Gracie, and Emmy Awards.

SARAH SILVERMAN

Sarah Silverman got her first break writing for *Saturday Night Live,* but was fired after one season for being "too Sarah Silverman." She played characters that were more her than them. In her first stand-up appearance at age seventeen, she sang a song entitled "Mammaries." She had roles on *Seinfeld, There's Something About Mary,* and *Rent,* but it was her 2005 stand-up feature film, *Jesus Is Magic,* that got people talking. Silverman's comedy attacks racial, sexual, and religious stereotypes with a razor-sharp dagger and turns it as it guts all of its victims.

"She came to the Belly Room to work out material. I enjoyed her humor. She's in an all- black room and holds her own." —Comedy Store promoter Nichelle Murdock

So it's no surprise she got into trouble when she said "chink" on *Conan O'Brien* in a satirical bit and refused to apologize when the Media Action Network for Asian Americans demanded one, saying she should've consulted with them first before doing the bit. Hey, isn't that type of thing covered in the First Amendment? Sarah thought so.

LISA LAMPANELLI

Publicly Lisa Lampanelli (born Lisa Lampugnale) has been on a career search for the perfect black man.

"My problem is, I can't get a good-looking white guy anymore. I just don't have the looks to get that. I can get hot blacks, but also blacks are now starting to get uppity and go for the skinny white ones and the Asians, which is very offensive to me that they don't stick with their roots—the chubby white girl!"

This frustration fuels the comedy of the Connecticut middle-class-raised Roman Catholic Italian who later became a journalist for *Rolling Stone, Spy,* and *Hit Parader.* She became a stand-up in 1990 and made a name for herself a decade later on the roasting circuit. To date she's been on the dais for Comedy Central's roasts of Pam Anderson, Flava Flav, William Shatner, Jeff Foxworthy, Denis Leary, and Donald Trump. Lampanelli has a resume that also includes comedy specials on HBO and Comedy Central, as well as movies and books. She says the reason she goes after black men is because white guys are too choosy. Lampanelli is married to a rock-and-roll club owner, was nominated for a Grammy for Best Comedy Album in 2008, and wrote a book, titled *Chocolate, Please: My Adventures in Food, Fat & Freaks.*

WHITNEY CUMMINGS

Whitney Cummings began like a number of comediennes— as a model. She used that money to pay for her college education, graduating with a degree in communications and film and a burning desire to run her mouth. She's performed on *The Tonight Show,* co-starred on *The Tony Rock Project,* appeared on *Chelsea Lately,* and toured nationally with Denis Leary. Her cred got more credible when her self-titled sitcom she created, co-produced, and stars in, *2 Broke Girls,* got picked up by NBC in 2011.

Television was always a great launching pad, but the new breed was reaping its benefits like never before. Whether it was behind the scenes or smack dab in front of the camera, it was the way to get remembered. Time had gone in reverse. There were now more channels than ever before, but also greater concentration from the viewing audience. If there was a network for what you specifically liked (and odds are there were unless you were really weird), then you were more than likely to be a loyal devotee of that network. Comedy Central got a strong dose of fan love when they took a chance with a scrawny comic named Dave and his brainchild, *Chappelle Show.* One of the many breakout personalities from that surprise hit was a comedienne named Dominique.

DOMINIQUE

The Washington, DC, native was as shocked at the show's success as anyone.

"I didn't know it was going to be almost iconic. To me, ever since the *Chappelle Show* been on, everybody's been in search of a *Chappelle Show* in some form or fashion. I was in the pilot episode and we were all like, 'I hope it gets picked up.' Boy, did it ever get picked up, but it was off the chain. I would've never thought it would've been the kind of show that it was."

Dominique remained a stand-up performer despite being on a successful television show. It's something many comedic performers wrestle with. Many drop off the stage to hit the mark and then adjourn to their dressing rooms or trailers. Not Dominique.

"If you're going to get into comedy, you gotta really, really grab it by the horns. To me, it's not easy. It's not gonna be easy. You gotta enjoy it. The ups and downs—you gotta count it all joy. You have high points, you have low points, but you gotta enjoy the journey."

Part of her journey's doing regular spots on Tom Joyner's morning radio show. Joyner would introduce her and she'd unleash on whatever the topic of the day might be, leaving the morning crew breathless after her rant, and then she'd be gone until the next airing. The gig was cool, the exposure great (Joyner was in syndication), but there was still something missing when it came to promoters.

"They call and they want me to be on the show because I do radio, but they don't want to pay like I do radio."

Her feelings about the stand-up comedy scene are just as pointed:

"I'm kind of from the old school. I'm from back in the day. So with the new comics, the lines got crossed for me. The new comics, to me, they on TV a little bit too early. They get different exposure in areas before they even found a voice. It kind of hurt comedy because the comics are in places, in my opinion, that they may not be ready for. I don't want to sound like, oh, I'm an old-school comic bashing the younger comics because I have sympathy for them because in a lot of ways it's not their fault.

"It's a process and you have to do who you are. That's what this thing is about—you got to do you.

"This, to me, is not a game of watching and studying, people going to comedy class, comedy school. What're you doing? Why are you going to comedy class and comedy school? Comedy class and comedy school is the stage and the microphone. Book a gig and figure this thing out. I'm not knocking the people that teach comedy class. Get your money on, but man, comedy class."

KYM WHITLEY

A former assistant to talk-show host Arsenio Hall, Kym Whitley didn't require a graduating degree to get into comedy. She also hadn't gone the tradition route of sleeping on couches and in cars to be successful in comedy. She did it by being funny in front of the right people at the right time. More of a comedic personality vs. being a comedienne, Whitley knows how to captivate an audience and definitely how to make them laugh.

"I've always called myself an improv comic. I'm a better improv comic than a regular stand-up. I used to hate saying the same jokes over and over again. I'm an off-the-cuff person."

There was many times Whitley's off-the-cuff-ness bordered on being offensive.

"This is what comics do. They're disrespectful."

They also have a reason for everything.

"If you notice all comics have ADD."

Whitley has appeared on television sitcoms, *The Parent 'Hood, Married . . . with Children, Moesha, That's So Raven,* and *The Parkers.* Her film credits include *Next Friday.* She's had her own talk show on BET, titled *Oh, Drama,* and Kym's a mainstay on the comedy circuit.

LUENELL

Being the youngest of eight children means this comedienne likes attention. As someone whose stage persona is completely unpredictable, this Arkansas native gets what she craves and then some. Having made her comedy reputation in Oakland, California, Luenell Campbell, known professionally as just Luenell, cracks up audiences with her signature short-cropped blond hair. As the prostitute in *Borat,* she stole the heart of theatrical audiences who would've sworn she was a real person in the mockumentary, not a really good actress. She pulled a similar artistic coup when appearing in Katt Williams's *American Hustle.* In that one, Luenell the actress once again seemed too real to be acting. Every time you turned around, Luenell was convincing us that she's a real girl, be it in *Californication, Wild N Out, All About Steve,* or the flood of motion pictures she's featured in.

LONI LOVE

Being omnipresent makes a funny comedienne a household name. TV makes a funny comedienne omnipresent. Being Loni Love means we won't get tired of your omnipresentness. The Detroit native was a long way from the Brewster-Douglass Housing Projects when she came in as runner-up on *Star Search* to the astonishment of the studio judges who proclaimed to the national audience that "Loni should've won" (the judges had to share the voting decision with the national audience voting block and they clearly disagreed with American's choice). Well, the loser went on to win in films (*Soul Plane*), television (practically every show on VH1), and stage (she tours over forty-five weeks annually). When she became a regular on *Chelsea Lately,* it was just another plateau in the rapid climb of a former Xerox engineer who gave up her day job on faith to pursue her passion and made the grateful comedy audience passionate about her. She did it, though not without incident and haters.

"When I came up, I didn't have anybody to turn to. Nobody would talk to me. All these comics, but there wasn't a lot of female comics to turn to. Definitely the male comics didn't think that I would be a serious comic or whatever. Nobody told me about the ups and downs and trials and tribulations of doing the road or handling clubs or doing television. They didn't. No one helped me."

Professional sexism was also always right around the corner.

"There are so few female headliners. I have to make sure when I'm booked for a club that I get everything I want before I even go to the club. So that's why it's important that things are put in my rider/contract. For example, I couldn't bring my own feature, and the problem with that is the clubs would just put anybody in front of me. Most of the time would be male comics, which that's not a problem. The problem is a lot of male comics have issues with having to go before a female. So they would do things like overdo their time, make a bad show, or whatever they could do. So I was able to fight them off by getting my own features with me because it's my own show now. It's a better show for my audience and me."

Being on TV regularly and having a high profile still didn't prevent financial discrepancies.

"When you're a road comic, they try not to pay the females as much as the male because they think people won't come to see the female."

However, when it came to some things, the club owners were more than happy to provide equal treatment.

"When I first started, they would have these comedy condos, and as a female, I mean, nobody really likes to be in those condos, but especially being a female, there are certain things that we go through during a month and you need a clean place. You need a safe place. You don't need a place where everybody has a key."

Things change with success, and those dumps quickly became a thing of the past as Loni moved rapidly up the ladder and made believers out of the last line of doubters.

Her energy, charm, and work ethic won over audiences and industry people alike. She was designated a role model and example of how hard work pays off. Loni herself credits those before her and how their sacrifices made her lifestyle and those of her peers possible.

"Because of comedy, I've been to all fifty states. I've been to Canada, South America—all because of performing. Because of comedy, I've been able to meet people I never thought I would meet in my lifetime. I've been able to actually be an opening act for people like Little Richard, Weird Al Yankovic, Anita Baker, Gladys Knight—people I grew up on. Because of comedy, I have my own radio show and I'm working with the rapper MC Lyte. All this happened because I took a step and decided I didn't want a traditional lifestyle and I'm able to do what I really like doing, which is trying to make people laugh and trying to make them forget their troubles for a little while."

Well, because of comedy the public has been treated to the talents of Loni Love and those like her. The Comedy Central special she did, titled *America's Sister,* couldn't have had a better name. Loni feels like family and we always look out for family.

CHELSEA HANDLER

Another yardstick for future comediennes is Chelsea Handler, who decided to become a stand-up comic after telling her DUI story to a group of other offenders, who found it hilarious. Her reform Judaism upbringing from her Mormon mother and Jewish father was the perfect combination of dysfunctionality to make Chelsea desire a life in the equally dysfunctional profession of show business. Starting out as an actress, she moved from New Jersey to Los Angeles at age nineteen to have a career. She's worked nationally as a comedian, was a regular on *Girl's Behaving Badly,* and a correspondent for *The Tonight Show.* In 2010, she became only the second woman to host the MTV Video Music Awards (the first was Roseanne

in '94) and her show, *Chelsea Lately,* has been a proven hit
for Comedy Central since 2007. She's a bestselling author,
a model, and a well-publicized mom. She "casually" dated
rapper 50 Cent and still had time to make *Forbes* magazine's
Celebrity Top 100.

*"All of this I really have to say not just because I'm on her
show, but this new thing of females in television has really
kinda got a boost because of Chelsea with her writing three
books; one of the books turned into a sitcom that's gonna be on
NBC. She's the only female in late night. Because of her, you
have this off-shoot—people are interested in females now."*
—Loni Love

The stage is set for a changing of the guard. If guys aren't
careful, the next book will be about how Phyllis Diller said
men aren't funny, that is, if any of the comediennes have
anything to say about it. As you can see, women have kept
the masses laughing for centuries, in all venues and in all
mediums. Though deterred and held back by their male
counterparts and the male power brokers, as well as by their
own kind, these determined ladies stayed the course and many
of the results are within these pages.

The major challenge for tackling this subject was the
number of women who've done comedy. For every legend
covered or unsung heroine unearthed, there will inevitably
be more omitted. So for every female from stage, radio,
voice-overs, film, television, and cyberspace who ever made
anybody laugh, we want to thank you for being comediennes.
You're part of a proud tradition wrought from sacrifice,
underestimation, and sheer will. Your kind has endured
personal hardship to bring joy to the public. You are one. You
are joyously unique. You are among the ranks of the new
breed of future starlets, divas, and icons. Comediennes such
as Neicy Nash, Shayla Rivera, Aisha Tyler, Maria Bamford,
Gina Yashere, Victoria Wood, Yvette Nicole Brown, Shappi
Khorsandi, B-Phlat, Lucy Porter, Cocoa Brown, Josie Long,

Sarah Millican, Karen Taylor, Tiffany Haddish, Tina Kim, Sara Contreras, Anjelah Johnson, Katy Flaming Brand, Lashelle Danee, Keisha Hunt, Olivia Lee, Dominique, Rosie Tran, Lady Roz, Iliza Shlesinger, Michelle Biloon, Julia Davies, D. D. Rainbow, Marlo, Ludo Vika, Kathleen Madigan, Simply Cookie, Janet Williams, Nicky Simone, Kate Clinton, Iva LaShawn, Janey Godley, Joyelle Johnson, Lynn Lavner, Aida Rodriguez, Pat Brown, Chaunte Wayans, Eve Webster, Daughne Keith, Ronnie Ancona, Jill Anenberg, Dawn French, Jo Brand, Nikki Carr, Felicia Michaels, Marga Gomez, Tammy Pescatelli, Shazia Mirza, Francesca Martinez, Jentle Phoenix, Linda Smith, Monique Marvez . . .

Appendix

Comedienne Q&A: Inside the Minds of Comediennes

You can write a book about comediennes, but nobody represents their point of view better than they do. No matter what the topic, ladies who make us laugh are always candid, poignant, and funny. Now that we've documented the history, the girls shared what it's like to be a comedienne. Are you ready for some females?

What is your biggest hurdle in comedy?

"Me not dreaming big enough, not believing big enough, not knowing that the greatest job that God could give you is being a comedienne." —Monique Marvez

"Myself. I'm my own worst enemy, my own worst critic. So it holds me back from doing things until I make sure it's perfect." —B-Phlat

"Getting past stereotypes." —Adele Givens

"I had to overcome the concept that pretty women couldn't be funny." —Ajai Sanders

"Being a woman and being of any ethnic group, because I think black comediennes and Latino comediennes, like myself, have two hurdles to jump. That's two strikes against you. The biggest strike against women to me is the perception that we're just not funny. That we only talk about tampons, and we only talk about screwing men and whatever. There's a whole lot more funny that comes out of females' mouths than we get credit for." —Shayla Rivera

"Comedy is hard for everyone. I don't ever say it's harder because I'm a woman." —Felicia Michaels

"The funnier I get, the broker I get." —Nikki Carr

"I have a really dirty sense of humor and have a really hard time writing clean." —Jill Anenberg

"Answering that question." —Vanessa Fraction

Have you ever had to downplay your femininity?

"The very first time I did comedy I purposely wore something where my titties . . . uh, cleavage—excuse me, cleavage— would be out. I said at least if they don't laugh, they ain't gonna boo me." —Vanessa Fraction

"I'm a big woman, so I didn't play down my femininity. I think that I became the nurturer. But then for those men that thought they were going to bully me, I became a gangstress."
—Thea Vidale

"I represent all average-size women. Ain't nothing wrong with going onstage fly and embracing who you are." —B-Phlat

"When I first started doing comedy, I thought I had to do comedy as a man in order to get respect. The more I got experience doing stand-up, I realized that there are certain things as a female I can do onstage that a male can't do. So now I've learned to embrace that." —Loni Love

"I believe a female comic loses a lot of her femininity because you're playing a boyish game, and if you don't play hardball with the boys, you're gonna get ran up the front and down the back." —Luenell

"Absolutely. In the beginning of your career we were jeans. I still wear jeans. You go up there with a tight dress on and your titties out—that's what they're looking at. That's what they focus on, and so you really gotta be hella funny."
—Kym Whitley

"I ain't gonna downplay nothing. I'm a girl and I like being a girl and there's nothing but boys in this business, especially when I came up. —Robin Montague

"My whole act is about I'm hot and here to hook up. It's a character who says I'm hot, but the whole act depends on me dressing down, because it's much funnier. I look at Phyllis Diller, who did downplay her figure to be funnier." —Henrietta

"I'm naturally a tomboy. I grew up with five brothers, so I've never been a girly girl. I can put on my lady when I want to."
—Iva LaShawn

"I think every female comedian should be true to themselves. I don't say I downplay my femininity, but I don't focus on it."
—Edwonda White

"Well, being a handsome woman, I'm there just to have brain sex with the audience and laugh until we cry, and that's it. I like to be in sneakers onstage because you never know when you might have to do a cartwheel or a split. I'm not doing it, but you just never know when you might have to." —Nikki Carr

How often has comedy demanded you to sacrifice time away from your family?

"Never! I don't think anyone becomes a comedienne because they have a normal, happy, unchallenged home life. So for years I booked myself on the holidays and significant days and wedding anniversaries so I wouldn't have to be there."
—Monique Marvez

"Out of fifty-two weeks I might have four to five weeks off. So basically I'm on the road at least forty-six weeks out of the year, and that's because of the level I'm at right now. You really have to go do the clubs to make a living as a comic." —Loni Love

"You miss a lot. My children, they went through a phase of being angry with me about it and then they saw the benefits. You see, I'd be missing shit not because I wasn't doing nothing. I was missing shit because I was working." —Thea Vidale

"It's something I never thought about till now. I'm trying to work smarter, not harder, because I'd really love to be home with my husband." —B-Phlat

"It's the sacrifice I have to make; out of sight, out of mind in the business." —Cocoa Brown

"Never! Comedy has never demanded anything from me. I do it willingly." —Adele Givens

Do you believe in mixing business with pleasure?

"It depends on the business and the pleasure." —Luenell

"I think that's our entire career." —Monique Marvez

"Absolutely—comedy is one of those careers where you just do that if you want the job." —Adele Givens

"I have dated comedians before, and it really didn't work out to my advantage based on the fact that I realized that when you date another performer, they become more like your competition rather than your counterpart." —Ajai Sanders

"I mentor a lot of young upcoming comediennes, and the first thing I tell them is if you're going to be with a comic, be with one. Don't be with all the comics on the circuit. So the answer to that would be 'no,' because you will not be considered serious and you'll lose focus." —Loni Love

"If I worked at IBM as a technology guru, I would probably not date my colleagues, so it's no different for me in comedy."
—Aida Rodriguez

"Aw, hell naw! Not in stand-up comedy." —Laura Hayes

"Sleeping with comics?! Hell no! Excuse my French. I don't shit where I eat." —Cocoa Brown

Where do you see yourself in five years?

"I just hope I end up eating nice-quality cat food and not the shit they have at Costco." —Felicia Michaels

If comedy disappeared in the morning, what are you qualified or prepared to do?

"That would be my job—how to get comedy back, because I need it." —Aida Rodriguez

"Go back to school and get my PhD and go on to be a professor in college." —Cocoa Brown

"I would be a child psychologist. I love kids and I have a real grip on how not to fuck 'em up." —Monique Marvez

"It's not the resume that gets the job; it's always the interview. Most comedians have a good personality, lighthearted and all that. So they are able to get in there and say the right things to get the job. I feel most comedians can probably get any job. I think that I could." —Edwonda White

"Offend people in a professional setting." —Jill Anenberg

"I never worry about my place in the business because I could always do something else in the business." —Hope Flood

"I'm a jack of all trades and a master of none. I can dig in the archives and make work because I know how to hustle."
—B-Phlat

"Still wouldn't have to work for nobody. I'd make my own money using my hands." —Nikki Carr

"I'm prepared to be the very best prostitute I could possibly be." —Kym Whitley

How has being a comedienne changed your life?

"It saved my life. It didn't change it, it saved it." —Monique Marvez

"When I date, I say, 'I'm in a serious love affair with comedy. You'll have to know that you are my jump-off.'" —Aida Rodriguez

"I've been able to vent and get rid of a lot of stress and pain and things that would've just had me in a corner depressed trying to slit my wrist." —Cocoa Brown

"I have the best job in the world as a female comedian. I'm living the dream. What I would do for free anyway—give my opinion, talk stuff, saying whatever I have to say—a lot of people do that, but I get paid for it." —Edwonda White

"The transition from full-time work—a 9-to-5, the rat race—to full-time comedienne, that's a struggle I never experienced, being broke like that before. I'm trying to tell people I'm new broke." —Vanessa Graddick

"Right now I should be working. Me and my sixteen-year-old daughter are living in a shelter. I should be getting a job, but no—I'm going to New York to do a show tomorrow night. When it picks up, it will pick up. We still roll through it. You know how comedy is? I don't want to get a job, then it picks up because I'm gone. I gotta be ready at all times." —Nikki Carr

"I got a chance to travel across the world in ways I could never imagine. I mean, it's taken me to places I never thought existed." —Ajai Sanders

"I'm more self-aware. I know my purpose as I get older. I'm more focused on what it is God has in store for me. So I just kind of take life slower and enjoy it more." —B-Phlat

"It has enhanced my confidence. Standing onstage in front of people is truly a way to build confidence." —Adele Givens

When you hear the word "comedienne," who comes to mind?

"I do." —Luenell

"Everybody. And I get upset at the same time. Like I love the word 'comedienne' to make it more feminine, but a comedian is a comedian and funny is funny." —Vanessa Graddick

"Sommore—who embodies femininity and feminine sexual power onstage, along with her funny. I think of Adele Givens and Simply Marvelous." —Aida Rodriguez

"Adele. Adele Givens." —Laura Hayes

"I would have to say Carol Burnett. Even though she claims to have not been a good stand-up comedienne, she always made me laugh." —Adele Givens

"Carol Burnett." —Monique Marvez

"Lisa Lampanelli, Sarah Silverman." —Jill Anenberg

"Wanda Sykes, Ellen DeGeneres, Paula Poundstone, Margaret Cho, Joan Rivers, Phyllis Diller, Mo'Nique, Whoopi Goldberg." —Alycia Cooper

"Gilda Radner was, to me, a comedienne. Carol Burnett was a comedienne. Vicki Lawrence, Whoopi Goldberg. Comedienne—I think of women, I guess, who had the whole gamut. A comedienne is a female comic who embodies everything. She uses her body, her mind, her spirit to bring the funny. She doesn't just limit herself to words and a microphone—shock value. She goes deeper than that. She gives you a piece of herself." —Cocoa Brown

What would you change about the comedy circuit?

"The way that there is a separate attitude in terms of support, women in comedy vs. men in comedy. I don't like the fact that a woman, who is just as funny, talented as a man, doesn't get as much propos. I know it's a man's world, but I don't have to like it." —Adele Givens

"Implement a union for comedians where they have health care, and they have a regulation on salary, the same thing like everybody else. Because we work harder than most people. We are the warriors and renegades of the night."
—Aida Rodriguez

"Comedy is the only entertainment genre that is non-unionized. We have no protection. We have no one to back us up if we get a bad check." —Luenell

"I would love for us to be able to have a governing body of ourselves, and if promoters didn't pay and do what they were supposed to do or club owners mistreated comics, there would be some resolve. I would make it where a lot of old-school comics could work more and I would create a circuit where comics could work two weeks straight and then go home and have some money in their pockets. I wouldn't nickel and dime 'em like people do. I would make sure we had some kind of union where we had money put away and health care, our own health care system of health care. SAG and AFTRA—they're not looking out for stand-up comics." —Thea Vidale

"I don't know if the band-together thing will work. It may for a small amount of time, but I don't think it'll work in the long run. People are at different levels in their careers and have accomplished different things that dictate that they make a few extra dollars." —Dominique

"One, I'd take it back to the old days, opener, middle, headliner. Two, you'd be a headliner, credits, TV, etc. you know headliner stuff. And I would book funny people, a black, white, Mexican, Jew, gentile, infidel, male, female, transgender, Muslim, midget." —Jus June

"Bring back the dead ones. The ones that was funny. I would educate people to go online and look up Rodney Dangerfield, Sid Caesar, Imogene Coca—people don't even know who they are. They were funny. Look at what was funny: slapstick is funny. Over the top is funny. Crazy is funny. Everything is way too flipping cool." —Henrietta

"Everybody just please be original. If I could lock people up for that, if we had, like, a comedy jail." —Nikki Carr

"I would create a shock treatment for anyone that steals anybody else's material. What we do is an art form, and when we dishonor someone else's work, it's like wearing a fake Gucci bag. It's not your stuff. If you can't afford the bag, then don't wear it." —Beth Payne

"I would like to change comedy audiences to have a little more sense in terms of what's comedy. They accept so much bad comedy." —Robin Montague

"People don't understand that comedy isn't simple. The easier a comedian makes it look, the more presence they have, the better they are, but that doesn't mean everybody can do it. But people find out all by themselves. Just give them the stage for five minutes. They will age."
—Shayla Rivera

"Stand-up should be more of a variety show. There's stand-ups with muppets. There's stand-ups that play the piano. Everybody's funny. Everybody ain't gotta hold the mike."

—Kym Whitley

"The clubs and promoters and all that would just respect the art of comedy more and pay people what they're worth."

—Vanessa Graddick

"I would sort of revamp the format of all-black comedy clubs. The white clubs have a certain formula and people can respect that. So audiences come in, they know what they're paying for; they know what they're getting. And I would make sure that the club owners actually pay the performers that they book."

—Ajai Sanders

"I'd create a filtering system. Comedy is just so saturated right now. The realness of it is kinda fading." —Vanessa Fraction

"It is the way it should be—everything. Because when you do any kind of art form, you have to put yourself at risk in order for your art to have truth to it." —Felicia Michaels

"Y'know what—I wouldn't change anything and I'll tell you why. I had a million answers pop in my head. So many club owners are wannabe comedians, so they're crappy to the comics 'cause they are envious. And you know those who can't do buy a club and are the house MC." —Monique Marvez

"I would change how comedy is actually being played out on television. *The Tonight Show* maybe has a comic once every two–three months. Because of that, people lose interest in comedy and in stand-up. We need more stand-up shows. Right now we're going back to that system of one comic is the hot comic. We don't have stand-up shows. People only know what they're used to. So you still have the older comics, but there's no place for the new comics to grow." —Loni Love

"Take away the color lines. No such thing as urban night. Make it funny. It doesn't matter if you're black, white, Latino—make these clubs open their doors to funny comedians and stop making it a race game." —Cocoa Brown

"I hate this 'Are you ready for a female?' What the fuck is that? I want to outlaw that." —Miss Laura Hayes

Who makes you laugh?

"Faceless, stupid open mikers." —Monique Marvez

"D'Militant's Facebook updates." —Aida Rodriguez

"Well, Roseanne makes me laugh. Joan Rivers makes me laugh." —Luenell

"Joan Rivers kills me. Margaret Cho is hilarious." —Rosie Tran

"George Carlin, Chris Rock, Martin Lawrence. I love old Moms Mabley. LaWanda Page in all her dirtiness. I love me some Joan Rivers." —Ajai Sanders

"Mo'Nique makes me crack up. Melanie Carmacho, people that are just dumb, crazy—act-stupid people, people who grew up really ignorant. I think the funniest people are the people the world doesn't know." —Kym Whitley

Who are your influences?

"Jonathon Winters and Richard Pryor. When he started out, he talked a lot about his neighborhood, the characters in his neighborhood, and he would turn into the characters as he told the stories of his youth. I think that struck a chord with me. That's how we always told stories in our family. We would turn into the characters we were talking about while telling the story. Lily Tomlin, of course, being on *Laugh-In,* and doing very specific characters. That was a strong influence with the first women of *Saturday Night Live* because they were part of this group of guys who were really powerful and yet they were still part of the group and in my eyes equal to them." —Nora Dunn

"Geraldine." —Sara Contreras

Do you love what you do? Why?

"Most of the time, when the business doesn't get in the way of the art." —Luenell

"I love it more than a man." —Thea Vidale

"More than breath." —Monique Marvez

"Comedy is a jealous boyfriend I like to call Ike, 'cause it beats the hell out of you every day, but I love it just the same."
—Cocoa Brown

Where do you get the inspiration for your jokes?

"I think about sex a lot, so I talk about it." —Vanessa Fraction

"I'm a very big observer. I can go to a room and sit in the cut and just never say a word and just observe everything and walk out with thirty minutes of material." —Cocoa Brown

What message do you want people to get from your comedy?

"That laughter, if not the best medicine, is right up there in the top two, right up there with oxycodone and something else you can't pronounce." —Adele Givens

"We don't have enough time to sit here and waste debating the things we should do in our lives. People need to do what they want to do." —Di Stanky

"If you're not happy doing something, then stop it."
—Vanessa Graddick

"Be true to yourself. Stop running from the truth. Accept truth. Stop trying to convince yourself it's something that it's not. If you need to change it, change it. But stop running from it."
—Cocoa Brown

"You're not alone and you can't mess it up."
—Monique Marvez

"Forget about their troubles for the few hours that they're in the comedy club and to have a good time because I think honestly and truly that is what our gift is from God; bless people through laughter. Everybody's ministry is not at church in the pulpit. This is our ministry. This is our gift from God." —Hope Flood

"Funny! I'm not trying to give a message. I'm not running for office." —Robin Montague

Do you feel you represent more than yourself when you perform (race, gender, etc.)?

"I represent comics, the art form, the respect for the science. I have one code: Laffter, that's the way you spell that; as my daddy would say, 'Talking loud and saying nothing,' that ain't my style of comedy." —Jus June

What advice do you have for anyone following in your footsteps?

"Don't do it, and then if they let that discourage them, that just said they didn't have what it takes anyway." —Luenell

"Don't think of themselves as comediennes, however you spell that. I'm just as funny with or without my vagaga, that's vagina. Second June says, 'Premise—set up—punch.'"

—Jus June

"Practice reading. Read as much as you can, 'cause I didn't. Go where your heart takes you. Find your style, and as soon as you have fun onstage, that's when you'll be successful."

—Kym Whitley

"Make sure you look at this industry as a business. Run it like a business. Incorporate yourself. Have a separate bank account. Track your expenses. File your taxes. Pay your quarterly expenses." —B-Phlat

"You've gotta ride the wave, the fluctuation of the monetary status. Sometimes you're up. Sometimes you're down. Sometimes you're down, down. Like right now we're basically at the bottom, but the way I teach my kids to look at it is, yeah, we down and we might be at the bottom, but when you hit the bottom, there's no place else to go but up."

—Nikki Carr

"To not gauge your success by the amount of television shows you've done or the exposure you've gotten. Gauge it by the audience reaction and make sure in your heart when you're on that stage you love it. If not, you might as well work at Payless." —Adele Givens

"Don't be afraid to expose yourself." —Jentle Phoenix

"Don't rush developing your own voice, but do get to a point in your career that you stop watching other people. Take your time finding your voice because once you've got it, it's who you are for the rest of your career." —Cocoa Brown

"Research as much as you can about this medium before you jump in. There's so much more to stand-up comedy than people realize." —Alycia Cooper

What do you think about comediennes being chosen as features for tours?

"The last thing you're supposed to do is be a female and funny and a beast all at the same time. They are scared to death of the formula, and the few that we are, we work on our own. We're outlaws. We're like hoes without pimps. We're outlaws."
—Cocoa Brown

What have you learned from comedy?

"I can't imagine my life without it, actually. That's how I relate to people. I'm an easier person to get along with. I've learned to laugh at so many things. That made life easier for me. I'm able to bear the things that go on in life. Comedy is my everything." —Vanessa Fraction

"I don't do comedy. Comedy is really who I am. Since I was a kid, my mother used to say, why you so silly all the time, but she never said stop acting silly. It's more who I am than what I do. So it's almost effortless." —Nikki Carr

"To not worry about the outcome. Just know that my lifestyle is of a comedienne with its ups and downs." —Felicia Michaels

How do you want to be remembered?

"Think of life as an ambience. You create a perfume around you. There's an ambience. There's energy. And my goal in life is whenever I leave a room, like a fragrance lingering, I want people to say I could've talked to that girl forever. I'm so sorry she left. What a great time we were having. I want to be a perfume." —Monique Marvez

"I want to be remembered as the light in the room. Wherever she went, she brought a light, and she had big titties. She should've had a breast reduction at thirty." —Kym Whitley

"Aw, man—you done took me all the way to my funeral. I want everybody to be broken apart." —Dominique

"Alive." —Miss Laura Hayes

Anything else you want to say?

"People don't respect the arts. You cannot live without art. Everything is art, even from the printing on the toilet paper."
—B-Phlat

"I love the comics that are so genius, when something's funny they will say, 'That's funny.' They don't actually laugh."
—Jentle Phoenix

"Plan B is for people who don't believe Plan A is gonna work."
—Aida Rodriguez

And there you have it!

Sources

Baker, Jean-Claude, and Chris Chase. 1993. *Josephine: The Hungry Heart*. New York: Random House.

Baker, Josephine, and Joe Bouillon Joe. 1977. *Josephine*. New York: Harper & Row.

Callwood, June. *The Naughty Nineties 1890/1900,* p. 79. Canada's Illustrated Heritage series. Natural Science of Canada Ltd.

Caper, William. 1999. *Whoopi Goldberg: Comedian and Movie Star*. Springfield, NJ: Enslow Publishers.

Diller, Phyllis, and Richard Buskin. 2005. *Like a Lampshade in a Whorehouse: My Life in Comedy*. New York: Penguin Group.

Edmonds, Andy. 1989. *Hot Toddy: The True Story of Hollywood's Most Sensational Murder*. New York: William Morrow and Co.

Gaines, Ann. 1999. *Whoopi Goldberg*. Philadelphia: Chelsea House.

Goldman, Herbert. *Fanny Brice: The Original Funny Girl*. Oxford University Press, 1993.

Grossman, Barbara. 1992. *Funny Woman: The Life and Times of Fanny Brice*. Indiana University Press.

Handler, Chelsea. 2008. *Are You There, Vodka? It's Me, Chelsea*. New York City: Simon Spotlight Entertainment.

Jackson, Carlton. 1990. *Hattie: The Life of Hattie McDaniel.* Lanham, MD: Madison Books.

Littleton, Darryl. 2006. *Black Comedians on Black Comedy: How African-Americans Taught Us to Laugh.* Applause Books.

Maltin, Leonard, and Richard W. Bann. 1977, rev. 1992. *The Little Rascals: The Life and Times of Our Gang.* New York: Crown Publishing/Three Rivers Press.

"Margaret Dumont Dies at 75. Acted in Marx Brothers Films." March 7, 1965. *The New York Times.*

Modjeska, Helena. 1894. *Women in Theater.* The World's Congress of Representative Women.

Rochlin, Margy. March 9, 2006. "Trying to Turn Elaine Into Christine." *The New York Times.*

Radner, Gilda. 1989. *It's Always Something.* New York: Simon and Schuster.

Rivers, Joan. *Bouncing Back.* 1997. HarperCollins.

———. 1986. *Enter Talking.* New York: Delacorte Press.

Smith, Dinitia. November 11, 1992. "Joy Shtick." *New York Magazine,* 50–51.

Watts, Jill. 2005. *Hattie McDaniel: Black Ambition, White Hollywood.* HarperCollins.

Wortis Leider, Emily. 2000. *Becoming Mae West.* Da Capo Press.

Photo Credits

The authors graciously acknowledge permission to reprint the following:

Beverly Nelson Collection, 2011

Booksearch.Blogspot.com, 2011

Classicmovieblog.com, 1918

Darryl Littleton Collection, 2011

En.Wikipedia.org, 1917

KPA Archival Collection, 1927

Laura Hayes Collection, 2011

Loni Love Collection, 2011

Luenell Campbell Collection, 2011

Northernstars.ca, circa 1920

Sheet Music Cover for "My Man," 1921

Sylvia Traymore Morrison Collection, 2011

Vanessa Fraction Collection, 2011

Index

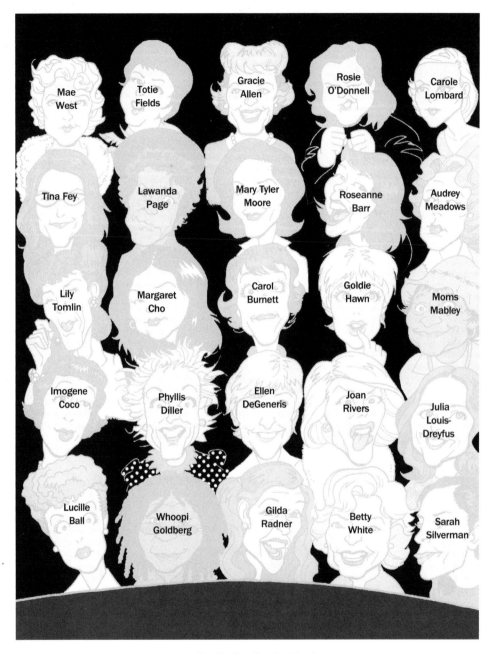

DISCARD